Alexander Mackenzie
and the Explorers of Canada

WORLD EXPLORERS

Alexander Mackenzie
and the Explorers of Canada

Georgia Xydes

Introductory Essay by Michael Collins

CHELSEA HOUSE PUBLISHERS

New York · Philadelphia

On the cover Mackenzie's map of his trek to the North Sea;
Thomas Lawrence's portrait of Alexander Mackenzie

Chelsea House Publishers
Editor-in-Chief Remmel Nunn
Managing Editor Karyn Gullen Browne
Copy Chief Mark Rifkin
Picture Editor Adrian G. Allen
Art Director Maria Epes
Assistant Art Director Howard Brotman
Series Design Loraine Machlin
Manufacturing Director Gerald Levine
Systems Manager Lindsey Ottman
Production Manager Joseph Romano
Production Coordinator Marie Claire Cebrián

World Explorers
Senior Editor Sean Dolan

Staff for ALEXANDER MACKENZIE AND THE EXPLORERS OF CANADA
Senior Copy Editor Laurie Kahn
Editorial Assistant Danielle Janusz
Picture Researcher Vicky Haluska
Senior Designer Basia Niemczyc

3 5 7 9 8 6 4

Library of Congress Cataloging-in-Publication Data

Xydes, Georgia.
    Alexander Mackenzie and the explorers of Canada/Georgia Xydes.
        p.   cm.—(World explorers)
    Includes bibliographical references and index.
    Summary: Examines the explorations of Sir Alexander Mackenzie
in Canada.
    ISBN 0-7910-1314-6
        0-7910-1539-4 (pbk.)
    1. Mackenzie, Alexander, Sir, 1763–1820—Juvenile literature.
2. Northwest, Canadian—Description and travel—To 1821—
Juvenile literature.   3. Northwest, Canadian—Discovery and
exploration—Juvenile literature.   4. Explorers—Northwest,
Canadian—Biography—Juvenile literature. [1. Mackenzie,
Alexander, Sir, 1763–1820. 2. Explorers. 3. Canada—Discovery
and exploration.] I. Title. II. Series.
                                                        91-42106

F1060.7.M1783X93   1992   CIP
971.2'01'0922—dc20   AC

CONTENTS

WORLD EXPLORERS

THE EARLY EXPLORERS

Herodotus and the Explorers of the Classical Age
Marco Polo and the Medieval Explorers
The Viking Explorers

THE FIRST GREAT AGE OF DISCOVERY

Jacques Cartier, Samuel de Champlain, and the Explorers of Canada
Christopher Columbus and the First Voyages to the New World
From Coronado to Escalante: The Explorers of the Spanish Southwest
Hernando de Soto and the Explorers of the American South
Sir Francis Drake and the Struggle for an Ocean Empire
Vasco da Gama and the Portuguese Explorers
La Salle and the Explorers of the Mississippi
Ferdinand Magellan and the Discovery of the World Ocean
Pizarro, Orellana, and the Exploration of the Amazon
The Search for the Northwest Passage
Giovanni da Verrazano and the Explorers of the Atlantic Coast

THE SECOND GREAT AGE OF DISCOVERY

Roald Amundsen and the Quest for the South Pole
Daniel Boone and the Opening of the Ohio Country
Captain James Cook and the Explorers of the Pacific
The Explorers of Alaska
John Charles Frémont and the Great Western Reconnaissance
Alexander von Humboldt, Colossus of Exploration
Lewis and Clark and the Route to the Pacific
Alexander Mackenzie and the Explorers of Canada
Robert Peary and the Quest for the North Pole
Zebulon Pike and the Explorers of the American Southwest
John Wesley Powell and the Great Surveys of the American West
Jedediah Smith and the Mountain Men of the American West
Henry Stanley and the European Explorers of Africa
Lt. Charles Wilkes and the Great U.S. Exploring Expedition

THE THIRD GREAT AGE OF DISCOVERY

Apollo to the Moon
The Explorers of the Undersea World
The First Men in Space
The Mission to Mars and Beyond
Probing Deep Space

CHELSEA HOUSE PUBLISHERS

Into the Unknown

Michael Collins

It is difficult to define most eras in history with any precision, but not so the space age. On October 4, 1957, it burst on us with little warning when the Soviet Union launched *Sputnik*, a 184-pound cannonball that circled the globe once every 96 minutes. Less than 4 years later, the Soviets followed this first primitive satellite with the flight of Yury Gagarin, a 27-year-old fighter pilot who became the first human to orbit the earth. The Soviet Union's success prompted President John F. Kennedy to decide that the United States should "land a man on the moon and return him safely to earth" before the end of the 1960s. We now had not only a space age but a space race.

I was born in 1930, exactly the right time to allow me to participate in Project Apollo, as the U.S. lunar program came to be known. As a young man growing up, I often found myself too young to do the things I wanted—or suddenly too old, as if someone had turned a switch at midnight. But for Apollo, 1930 was the perfect year to be born, and I was very lucky. In 1966 I enjoyed circling the earth for three days, and in 1969 I flew to the moon and laughed at the sight of the tiny earth, which I could cover with my thumbnail.

How the early explorers would have loved the view from space! With one glance Christopher Columbus could have plotted his course and reassured his crew that the world was indeed round. In 90 minutes Magellan could have looked down at every port of call in the *Victoria's* three-year circumnavigation of the globe. Given a chance to map their route from orbit, Lewis and Clark could have told President Jefferson that there was no easy Northwest Passage but that a continent of exquisite diversity awaited their scrutiny.

In a physical sense, we have already gone to most places that we can. That is not to say that there are not new adventures awaiting us deep in the sea or on the red plains of Mars, but more important than reaching new places will be understanding those we have already visited. There are vital gaps in our understanding of how our planet works as an ecosystem and how our planet fits into the infinite order of the universe. The next great age may well be the age of assimilation, in which we use microscope and telescope to evaluate what we have discovered and put that knowledge to use. The adventure of being first to reach may be replaced by the satisfaction of being first to grasp. Surely that is a form of exploration as vital to our well-being, and perhaps even survival, as the distinction of being the first to explore a specific geographical area.

The explorers whose stories are told in the books of this series did not just sail perilous seas, scale rugged mountains, traverse blistering deserts, dive to the depths of the ocean, or land on the moon. Their voyages and expeditions were journeys of mind as much as of time and distance, through which they—and all of mankind—were able to reach a greater understanding of our universe. That challenge remains, for all of us. The imperative is to see, to understand, to develop knowledge that others can use, to help nurture this planet that sustains us all. Perhaps being born in 1975 will be as lucky for a new generation of explorer as being born in 1930 was for Neil Armstrong, Buzz Aldrin, and Mike Collins.

The Reader's Journey

William H. Goetzmann

This volume is one of a series that takes us with the great explorers of the ages on bold journeys over the oceans and the continents and into outer space. As we travel along with these imaginative and courageous journeyers, we share their adventures and their knowledge. We also get a glimpse of that mysterious and inextinguishable fire that burned in the breast of men such as Magellan and Columbus—the fire that has propelled all those throughout the ages who have been driven to leave behind family and friends for a voyage into the unknown.

No one has ever satisfactorily explained the urge to explore, the drive to go to the "back of beyond." It is certain that it has been present in man almost since he began walking erect and first ventured across the African savannas. Sparks from that same fire fueled the transoceanic explorers of the Ice Age, who led their people across the vast plain that formed a land bridge between Asia and North America, and the astronauts and scientists who determined that man must reach the moon.

Besides an element of adventure, all exploration involves an element of mystery. We must not confuse exploration with discovery. Exploration is a purposeful human activity—a search for something. Discovery may be the end result of that search; it may also be an accident, as when Columbus found a whole new world while searching for the Indies. Often, the explorer may not even realize the full significance of what he has discovered, as was the case with Columbus. Exploration, on the other hand, is the product of a cultural or individual curiosity; it is a unique process that has enabled mankind to know and understand the world's oceans, continents, and polar regions. It is at the heart of scientific thinking. One of its most significant aspects is that it teaches people to ask the right questions; by doing so, it forces us to reevaluate what we think we know and understand. Thus knowledge progresses, and we are driven constantly to a new awareness and appreciation of the universe in all its infinite variety.

The motivation for exploration is not always pure. In his fascination with the new, man often forgets that others have been there before him. For example, the popular notion of the discovery of America overlooks the complex Indian civilizations that had existed there for thousands of years before the arrival of Europeans. Man's desire for conquest, riches, and fame is often linked inextricably with his quest for the unknown, but a story that touches so closely on the human essence must of necessity treat war as well as peace, avarice with generosity, both pride and humility, frailty and greatness. The story of exploration is above all a story of humanity and of man's understanding of his place in the universe.

The WORLD EXPLORERS series has been divided into four sections. The first treats the explorers of the ancient world, the Viking explorers of the 9th through the 11th centuries, and Marco Polo and the medieval explorers. The rest of the series is divided into three great ages of exploration. The first is the era of Columbus and Magellan: the period spanning the 15th and 16th centuries, which saw the discovery and exploration of the New World and the world ocean. The second might be called the age of science and imperialism, the era made possible by the scientific advances of the 17th century, which witnessed the discovery

of the world's last two undiscovered continents, Australia
and Antarctica, the mapping of all the continents and
oceans, and the establishment of colonies all over the
world. The third great age refers to the most ambitious
quests of the 20th century—the probing of space and of
the ocean's depths.

As we reach out into the darkness of outer space and
other galaxies, we come to better understand how our
ancestors confronted *oecumene,* or the vast earthly unknown. We learn once again the meaning of an unknown
18th-century sea captain's advice to navigators:

> And if by chance you make a landfall on the shores of
> another sea in a far country inhabited by savages and
> barbarians, remember you this: the greatest danger and the
> surest hope lies not with fires and arrows but in the
> quicksilver hearts of men.

At its core, exploration is a series of moral dramas. But it
is these dramas, involving new lands, new people, and
exotic ecosystems of staggering beauty, that make the explorers' stories not only moral tales but also some of the
greatest adventure stories ever recorded. They represent
the process of learning in its most expansive and vivid
forms. We see that real life, past and present, transcends
even the adventures of the starship *Enterprise.*

A Murderer's Fancy

As the fire died down again, a few sparks from the last log floated upward into the dim, damp room. In the corner the frost crept back along the crevices in the rough bark covering the log walls, and the shaggy hide over the low door grew stiff in the deep cold of the night. Finally, the younger man stirred enough to reach for another small log in the corner. As he placed it slantwise on the scorched timbers in the fireplace, they collapsed into an orange-red heap of flaring embers, and the sudden glow illuminated the man's handsome face in the darkening room. No longer a youth, he was still young, with curly light-brown hair and bright, intelligent eyes. In his speech were evident traces of the burr of his native Scotland, but he was many thousands of miles away from home.

Outside, around the tiny cabin and its flickering fire, spread hundreds of thousands of acres of thick, dark forest, made up of pine, fir, and spruce, interspersed here and there with treacherous muskeg, watered by numerous raging and unexplored rivers and several tremendous lakes, peopled by a number of Indian nations, and inhabited by an overwhelming abundance of fur-bearing animals. Located some 30 miles south of Lake Athabasca, on the Athabasca River, near the upper reaches of the borders of the present-day Canadian provinces of Alberta and Saskatchewan, the rude dwelling constituted the northernmost and westernmost outpost of the dauntless fur traders of the North West Company (NWC). As such, it also constituted the northernmost and westernmost extent of

Sir Alexander Mackenzie, as painted sometime around 1800 by Thomas Lawrence, court painter to King George III of England. This portrait is one of the few existing likenesses of the celebrated fur trader and explorer of western Canada done from life.

The history of the exploration of Canada is in large part the history of the fur trade. The fur trade's importance to Canada is indicated by this illustration, which graced a 1777 map of the region. Defining features of Canada's rugged landscape, such as forest, rivers and lakes, and mountains are shown, as is the linchpin of its economy—an Indian exchanging furs for goods with a trader.

the ongoing overland exploration of the continent of North America and the sprawling wilderness expanse that would become the nation of Canada.

The younger man, Alexander Mackenzie by name, turned now to face his much older companion, who continued their conversation in a low rumble. For many long, dark winter days in early 1788 they had talked back and forth in front of their primitive hearth, discussing Indian customs, the price of beaver fur, and, most of all, exploration. A tenuous understanding, sometimes approaching friendship, now existed between the two men. "Thus far my neighbor and I have agreed very well and I believe we shall continue on the same good footing for the season," Mackenzie wrote to his cousin Roderick McKenzie. Two men icebound for at least two-thirds of a year in a cabin some hundreds of miles away from other companions might have hoped for warmer relations between them, but even peaceful coexistence constituted a kind of triumph.

Mackenzie was now 24 years old, and his essential character was well formed. Lordly, imperious, haughty, stoic, and reserved, he was a man of few words under most circumstances, but while keeping company with his cabinmate he had good reason to guard his tongue, for those who disagreed with Old Peter Pond had an unnerving way of winding up dead. Sometime in the early 1770s, while Pond was serving his apprenticeship in the fur trade in and around a small trading post—called Detroit—strategically located between Lake Erie and Lake Huron, an argument with another trader led to a sunrise duel. As Pond, with his idiosyncratic spelling and usage, put it: "We met the next morning eairley and discharged pistels in which the pore fellow was unfortenat." Pond said that he reported the killing, but the long arm of the law did not reach to the fur trader's outposts. "Thare was none to prosecute me," he wrote.

Nevertheless, Pond thought it best to put some distance between himself and the scene of the unfortunate incident. Shortly after the outbreak of the American Revolution, he headed for Canada and the northwest country, as the vast territory beyond Hudson Bay was known. There, a host of independent operators and small trading concerns were busily seeking new regions in which to trade their goods— axes, ice chisels, knives, files, flints, guns, ammunition, copper kettles, cloth, glass beads, tobacco, and alcohol— to the Indians in exchange for beaver skins and the furs of other animals. The motive for the wanderings of these rugged individuals was always profit, but these "pedlars," as the men of the Hudson's Bay Company (HBC) derisively referred to their mostly Scottish competitors, were also the first explorers of western Canada, and it was their ramblings that revealed the geographic secrets of its immensely vast landscape. Within a short time, Pond fell in with Simon McTavish, the forceful visionary who merged the pedlars into the shifting partnership known to history as the North West Company.

In 1778, backed by McTavish, three brothers named Frobisher, and two siblings named McGill (whose profits from the fur trade, made possible in large part by Pond's daring and expertise, would fund the establishment of McGill University, one of Canada's foremost centers of learning), Pond hazarded a trip to the Athabasca region, which was then known only by Indian reports portraying it as unimaginably rich in game. The word *Athabasca* had dominated the campfire conversation of Canada's fur trappers for years, holding for them the same mythical allure that the legend of El Dorado had once held for the Spanish conquistadores.

With 16 voyageurs manning 5 canoes heavily laden with tons of supplies and trade goods, Pond left Cumberland House, the NWC post on the North Saskatchewan River, in the spring of 1778. A series of short portages between numerous small streams and lakes took him northward to the Churchill River, which he and his men then paddled up as far north as the Methy Portage, a 12-mile valley separating the Churchill and the Clearwater River, as well as the Hudson Bay and Arctic river systems. The north end of the portage is a 700-foot cliff overlooking the Clearwater. After scrambling to the top of this cliff, canoes and supplies in tow, Pond and his hardy voyageurs were the first white men to behold this magnificent vista, which overlooks a wooded valley and is still celebrated for its beauty. From there, the going was much easier, westward down the Clearwater and northward down the Athabasca River. About 30 miles south of Lake Athabasca, Pond called a halt, and he and his men threw up several cabins. That winter, he traded his goods with the Chipewyan Indians; by spring, he had twice as many prime beaver pelts as his canoes could carry. His arrival back at Cumberland House caused a sensation, and he was rewarded with a partnership in the North West Company.

But Pond's temperament would constantly cause problems for both himself and those with whom he came in contact. He was placed in charge of the Athabasca outpost, but while journeying there in the autumn of 1781, the premature freezing of the northern waterways—the Canadian fur trader's highways—forced him to winter at Lac La Ronge, where a colleague named Étienne Waden was in residence. Waden was the head of an NWC faction that opposed granting the Athabasca district to Pond, and a dinner meeting between the two rivals ended with Waden sprawled on the floor, dead from several gunshot wounds. Sometime after the springtime thaw, Pond and a subordinate who had also attended the bloody supper were taken back to Montreal and tried. Although both were somehow acquitted, "their innocence was not so apparent as to extinguish the original suspicion," as a fellow trader put it.

Despite his acknowledged ability as a trader, which owed in large part to his sympathetic treatment of the Indians, and the service he had done it by exploring the Athabasca region, which would shortly become the company's most profitable district, Pond was voted a reduced share in the North West Company at the next meeting of its senior partners. (Such reorganizations of the NWC were commonplace.) The company would often use brutal means to defend its territory against competitors, but killing one's own was generally frowned upon. Pond's quest for more influence within the company also suffered because he invested very little capital in it.

Still, after a brief self-imposed exile in the United States, Pond retained control of Athabasca. Most of his colleagues in the fur trade gave him a very wide berth; he was described as "odd in his manner" with a "violent temper and unprincipled character." There was another murder; after an argument with Pond, a rival trader, John Ross, was found shot to death, although Pond was never definitely fingered as the culprit. Few men would agree to winter with him, but Mackenzie, as one of the youngest and least influential partners of the freewheeling, loosely organized North West Company, had little choice. Besides, the younger man was nothing if not ambitious, and it was understood that he was being groomed to succeed Pond as the head of their remote outpost whenever the older man's eccentricities and propensity for violence at last forced his ouster from the company. (As it turned out, that event would take place the very next spring.)

The various styles of winter headgear for which beaver fur was used in the Canadian city of Quebec may be seen in this drawing from 1805. The wrapping at top left was worn by someone concerned more with warmth than style; the figure at bottom right is wearing a more fashionable beaver. At bottom left one sees the kind of beaver hat worn by soldiers; at top right is an Indian headdress made of beaver fur. The variety of styles of beaver hats worn in Europe was even greater.

More than his erratic character made Pond an anomaly among the Nor'Westers, as the men of the fledgling North West Company referred to themselves. At 48 years of age, Pond was ancient to still be working as a wintering partner—that is, a shareholder who spent his winters manning one of the "Great Company's" far-flung trading posts south and west of Hudson Bay, where its great rival, the Hudson's Bay Company, maintained its century-old monopoly on the fur trade, rather than figuring profits in the company's countinghouses in far-off Montreal and tippling to excess at the legendarily boisterous gatherings of the Beaver Club. (Membership in the Beaver Club was limited to those who had spent at least one full winter in *le pays d'en haut*—the high or north country, as the Nor'Westers referred to the rivers, lakes, and forests of the interior where their men were stationed.) Few men voluntarily subjected themselves to such a life—with its severe isolation, its extreme climate, and all its other attendant hardships—for very long. Whatever his other character flaws, Pond's endurance made him special even among men renowned for their hardiness.

Pond also stood out because he was an American, born (in 1740) and raised in Milford, Connecticut, where his father had hoped he would carry on the family shoemaking business. Virtually all of the partners in the North West Company—a number that fluctuated constantly but peaked at 36—were Scotsmen. Moreover, as the historian Peter C. Newman has pointed out, virtually all of them were related, either by birth or marriage. In the company's approximately 40-year history, there were 4 different Finlays, 5 Camerons, 6 McTavishes, 7 McLeods, 7 Simon Frasers, 8 McGillivrays, 14 Grants, and 14 McKenzies among its partners. The McDonalds were simply too numerous to count and found it necessary to distinguish themselves by including their place of origin in their surname, as in John McDonald of Perth. Pond's wintering mate, Alexander Mackenzie, was tied to the company hierarchy in this fashion. His first cousin Roderick McKenzie married the daughter of the fur trader Charles Chaboillez, whose other daughter was married to Simon McTavish, the company's founder and dominant genius. McTavish alone had three nephews, two grandnephews, three nephews-in-law, two brothers-in-law, three first cousins, and one distant cousin within the company.

What most set Pond apart from his fellow Nor'Westers, however, especially the senior partners in their palatial mansions back in Montreal, was his curiosity, for in his untutored way, Pond was quite the geographer. Not that the company was hidebound in its approach to the fur trade; far from it. The North West Company was on the verge of becoming the dominant force in the Canadian fur trade because its adventurous men, unlike their staid counterparts on Hudson Bay, had been relentless in pushing into the Canadian interior in search of new lands where they could obtain furs and pelts. None had been more daring than Pond, but his eagerness to learn about the lands even farther west and north of Athabasca was matched by only one Nor'Wester—his reticent protégé, Alexander Mackenzie.

It was this shared curiosity about the geography of the westernmost expanses of Canada that enabled Pond and Mackenzie to forge a bond. By the flickering light of candles and the fire in the hearth, the grizzled American murderer showed the upright young Scotsman a chart he had been working on during his winters in Athabasca, an amalgamation of the little solid information available about Canada's remaining unknown lands and what snippets he could gather from the Indians. Somewhere to the west, Pond knew, the great English sea captain and explorer James Cook, in exploring along the northwest coast of the continent in the course of his third and final circumnavigation of the world, had discovered an inlet of the Pacific Ocean that mingled with fresh water from the interior. Based on what he had been told by the Indians (or what he understood them to have said), Pond contended that this inlet was in fact the mouth of a "great river" that he believed trended westward from the Great Slave Lake, a body of water about 150 miles north of Lake Athabasca and connected to it by the Slave River. The veteran trapper believed that it would take only 6 days' paddling—a voyage of about 200 miles—down this river to reach the Pacific.

Mackenzie was fascinated, for he instantly grasped the ramifications for the fur trade of what Pond was telling him. The greatest obstacle the Nor'Westers faced in their competition with the Hudson's Bay Company was the length of their supply lines. By canoe, along the established river and lake routes plied by its voyageurs, it was some 4,000 miles from Lake Athabasca to the company head-

quarters in Montreal, on the St. Lawrence River, a distance that had to be traversed in the 4 ice-free months between mid-May and mid-September. From Montreal, which was itself accessible by water only a few months out of the year, the furs gathered by traders in the west then had to travel four more months across the Atlantic to be sold in London. The goods traded by the pedlars to the Indians for furs had to travel a voyage of similar length and duration from England to Montreal to Athabasca. Although unavoidable, such a transportation system was at best unwieldy and inefficient, for it meant that the Montreal fur merchants had to finance and store trade goods for two years before seeing a return on their investment, as it was not possible for even the most indefatigable voyageurs to make a round trip by canoe between

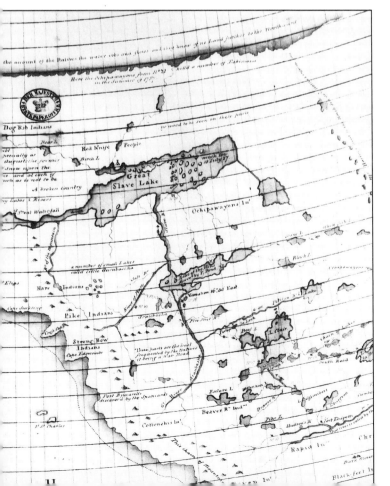

Peter Pond's map of western Canada. Pond's great river of the West is the watercourse he has drawn trending westward from the Great Slave Lake. Although he left it uncharted beyond what he has labeled a "great waterfall," it is evident that he believed it to be only a short distance from both the Pacific Ocean and "Cook's R[iver]." Note also that Pond has the Rocky Mountains stopping just south of his river.

Athabasca and Montreal (or vice versa) in the short time between the arrival of the supply ships from London sometime after the spring breakup and their departure before the onset of the winter freeze. In this regard, the HBC men had the great advantage, for a ship could make the voyage between London and the roadstead off York Factory, the HBC headquarters at the mouth of the Nelson River, in less than four months, and the HBC's outposts were all in close enough proximity to Hudson Bay that goods and furs could be exchanged within the same short summer season.

Easy access from Athabasca via water to a warm-water port on the Pacific would therefore greatly simplify things for the Nor'Westers. It would also, in essence, give the North West Company control of a northwest passage, as the long-sought water route linking the Atlantic and Pacific oceans across North America was called, allowing the Great Company, as Mackenzie envisioned, to transform the North American fur trade into a truly global commercial enterprise. During his reconnaissance of the Northwest, Cook had traded hatchets, flints, and various metal goods to the Indians of Nootka Sound, off Vancouver Island, for sea otter pelts. The great British mariner would be killed in Hawaii less than a year later, but on their return voyage his men put in at the port of Canton, in China, where the sea otter pelts fetched tremendous prices. If Pond's maps were right, Mackenzie believed, the North West Company would be able to expand the fabulously lucrative fur trade to the Far East, with greater profits for all its shareholders, including himself.

So night after night he pondered the charts his murderous mentor had drawn, while Pond rambled on, explaining that the tremendous stony mountains to the west—known today as the Rocky Mountain Range—ended south of his great river, allowing it unimpeded access to the ocean. With each examination of Pond's crude

PERSEVERANCE

The coat of arms of the North West Company. The Nor'Westers were every bit as persevering and industrious as the animal whose fur they sought so relentlessly.

map, with each repetition by Pond of his geographic theories, Mackenzie's excitement mounted. When at last the ice on the river began to break up with the arrival of the late north-country spring, Mackenzie and Pond set off upriver to make the two-month journey to the annual meeting of the wintering partners and their Montreal counterparts at Grand Portage, on the western shore of Lake Superior. As always, they made an unlikely duo. Pond, disillusioned, would never return to le pays d'en haut. Mackenzie, who could not wait to get the approval of the company's senior partners for his proposed expedition to the Pacific, was just beginning the career that would make him the greatest of the explorers of Canada.

A Monopoly on Furs

Alexander Mackenzie was born on the island of Lewis with Harris, one of the Outer Hebrides, sometime in 1764. Some chroniclers give his birthplace as Stornoway, the chief fishing port and largest town on the island, but that is uncertain. Likewise, little is known about his family and their background except that the Mackenzies, according to some sources, were "prominent." Whatever the family's social status, the 18th century was a time of great poverty for most of the residents of the Hebrides, which are a chain of some 500 small islands off the west coast of Scotland. Either because of economic troubles or the desire to make a new start in a place of less painful memories and associations, Mackenzie's father brought his oldest son—Alexander had a brother and two sisters—to North America in 1775 following the death of his wife.

The family arrived just months before the outbreak of the American Revolution. They settled first in New York, where Mackenzie's father joined a Loyalist regiment (Loyalists were those who, as opposed to the independence-minded American rebels, retained their loyalty to Great Britain) and eventually remarried. Young Alexander was therefore raised by two aunts, for a time in the Mohawk Valley and then in Canada, probably in Montreal.

A trading-room scene at a Hudson's Bay Company (HBC) outpost, where goods ranging from colored beads to blankets to hatchets, thimbles, and guns could be obtained in exchange for made-beavers.

The fishing village of Stornoway, seen here in the early part of the 19th century, was most likely the birthplace of Alexander Mackenzie in 1764. Stornoway is on the island of Lewis with Harris, one of the Outer Hebrides.

Though he most likely received little better than a rudimentary education, he nonetheless possessed a keen intelligence and a fierce ambition, which he began to put to work for the Montreal fur-trading firm of Finley, Gregory & MacLeod in 1779, when he was just 15 years old. For the next five or six years he worked in the firm's countinghouse and warehouse, with occasional forays to its outposts on the Great Lakes and even as far as Ile-a-la-Crosse, far west of Hudson Bay on the Churchill River. In this fashion, he learned virtually every aspect of the business; his aptitude so impressed founding partner John Gregory that when his firm merged with the hard-driving North West Company in or around 1785, Mackenzie was brought along and given one full partnership share. It made the young man a very minor partner, but it was a significant concession nonetheless. It was the same ownership stake controlled, for example, by Peter Pond, who had been in the trading business for twenty-some years. And within a few short years, Mackenzie had been posted to the Athabasca district—the most remote and profitable of the North West Company's far-flung outposts.

Mackenzie had joined the North West Company at a critical time in the history of the Canadian fur trade. For almost 100 years, beginning in 1670, the Hudson's Bay Company had enjoyed a virtual monopoly on the commerce in pelts from the Canadian interior. That year, a group of 19 investors—foremost among them Prince Rupert of the Rhine, printmaker, chemist, inventor, military scourge of the Puritans, and cousin of Charles II, king of England—formed a partnership for the purpose of investing in the fur trade. On May 2, 1670, Charles awarded to the "Company of Adventurers of England tradeing into Hudsons Bay" a charter that granted them, as "true lords and proprietors," the "sole Trade and Commerce" in and around Hudson Bay. The full geographic extent of the territory granted the Adventurers included all the land adjoining every river and stream that drained into the bay. Prince Rupert's Land, as this tremendous expanse was known, therefore encompassed 1.5 million square miles— almost twice the area of western Europe. It constituted 40 percent of present-day Canada, including northern Ontario and Quebec, all of Manitoba, much of southern Saskatchewan and Alberta, much of the eastern portion of the Northwest Territories, and a large part of the U.S. states of Minnesota and North Dakota. In exchange, the company was obligated to pay a rent of the skins of "two elks and two black beavers" to the monarch "whensoever and as often as wee our heirs and successors shall happen to enter into the said Countryes Territoryes and Regions hereby granted."

Within four weeks of the granting of the charter, the first HBC ships set sail for Hudson Bay. Within a few years, the company had begun to establish its network of fortified trading posts—called often "factories" or "houses," as in York Factory or Rupert House—at the mouths of rivers on the south end of Hudson Bay. In

1672, the first sale of HBC furs was held, at Garraway's Coffee House in London. The riotous bidding on a specific lot of furs was conducted during the time it took a one-inch candle to burn down; the high bidder at the moment the flame finally guttered out took the pelts. The auction and its yearly successors were a smashing success, although poet laureate John Dryden, a cynical guest at the first sale, decried in verse the spirit of commercialism that prevailed:

> Friend, once 'twas fame that led thee forth,
> To brave the tropic heat: the frozen North.
> Later 'twas gold. Then beauty was the spur.
> Now our gallants venture but for fur.

The Adventurers did not much care if poets found fur aesthetically unacceptable as an impetus for their efforts. Within a decade of the first sale, the Hudson's Bay Company was earning a yearly profit of 200 percent. And because the company enjoyed a monopoly, it did not have to work overly hard for its money. In essence, its salaried employees simply waited in their bayside fortresses for the spring thaw to break up the ice on the rivers so that the Indians—mainly the Cree but also the Chipewyan and the Assiniboin—could paddle their canoes downriver and exchange the furs they had gathered for a variety of goods, chief among them copper kettles and cookware, muskets, knives, axes, flannel, wool, and the famed HBC blankets.

Although the Indians did all the hard labor of trapping and preparing pelts, life at a company outpost was seldom easy or enjoyable for an HBC employee. All the Bay men—the company's in-country employees—were on salary, even the chief factor, or governor, of an outpost. Only the original investors and their successors owned shares in the company, and none of them ever set foot in Canada. The company was a rigid hierarchy, divided into servant (laborers, such as carpenters, net menders, cooks, blacksmiths, stevedores, fishermen, hunters, firewood cutters, snow shovelers, minor clerks, and general apprentices) and officer classes, within which there were various distinctions of superiority. "Everybody found reason to be grateful for superiority over someone else," wrote Philip Goldring, a historian of the company. Loyalty and perseverance were required to climb this ladder; 13 to 20 years of service as a clerk, the lowest officer's rank, was generally required before promotion to the position of chief trader, with the corresponding responsibility for conducting the actual bartering at a post. Above the chief trader was the chief factor, who made the day-to-day decisions about running the post, although all policy matters were decided by its London directorate, which consisted of seven committee-men, a deputy governor, and the governor. Although the various chief factors on Hudson Bay were often called governors, there was only one Governor. Prince Rupert was the first, though none is more well known than Lord John Churchill, the first duke of Marlborough, one of the

In this 1768 engraving, entitled Inhabitants of North America, Near Hudsons Bay, with Their Manner of Killing Wild Fowl, *the unknown artist has made the Native Americans of the region, with their full, bushy beards, closely resemble Europeans. The dwelling at right more closely resembles an army tent than it does any Indian or Inuit dwelling near Hudson Bay.*

greatest military commanders in history and an exceptionally savvy head of the company.

Those willing to commit such a portion of their life to a company notoriously parsimonious with its salaries spent their days in any of a number of crudely constructed log redoubts and shelters spread out around Hudson Bay. The outposts were "forts" only in theory; although ostensibly planned with defense in mind and usually guarded by cannons, their construction was haphazard at best and they could be easily taken by anyone foolhardy enough to want them. Four walls of log palisades constituted the exterior; the officers' quarters and a bachelors' hall occupied the central courtyard, with the living quarters of the servants thrown up against the outside walls. Various storage sheds and warehouses also cluttered the interior.

The living quarters offered only a minimum of protection against the fierceness of the nine-month Hudson Bay winter, which matches in severity any climate known on earth. Temperatures regularly hover in the range of −40°F, and much lower measurements have been recorded. Within a few weeks of the onset of winter, all the interior walls and even the planks of beds would be coated

York Factory, near the confluence of the Hayes and Nelson rivers at Hudson Bay, was the first permanent HBC trading station. It was founded in the 1680s; at its height, in the mid-19th century, it was a veritable small town of 30 buildings, laid out in an H, including a hospital, an Anglican church, a library, a smithy, a bakery, and officers' and servants' living quarters.

with a sheet of ice. During the day, the heat from the crude brick stoves inside would melt some of this buildup, but once the fires were banked at night, the runoff would immediately freeze once more. The result was an exceptionally unhealthy mixture of constant, deadly cold and unavoidable dampness. The stoves were little consolation; although they provided a welcome source of heat, their chimneys worked imperfectly. During winter, all windows were boarded up with three-inch shutters; at night, the chimney grates would be sealed off so as to retain every bit of the fast-diminishing heat of the fire. The result was that the interior rooms of an HBC outpost were typically choked with thick smoke as well as coated with ice. Outside, snow often piled up higher than the buildings themselves.

To protect himself, the Bay man donned a cuffed outer cloak made of moose skin. A cape made of the fur of a fox, marten, or beaver was draped around the shoulders; pants made from deerskin and lined with flannel clad the legs. Underlying all, closest to the skin, were three layers of cut-up blankets. Footgear consisted of thick leather wrapped and tied tightly around the instep. This was indoor wear. To step outside to fetch wood or hunt, Bay men added a beaver skin around their neck and shoulders, a scarf or neck wrapping made by sewing two complete skins of a white fox together at the tails, moose-skin boots, and snowshoes that measured more than four feet in length. The exoticism of their appearance was increased by the difficulty of maintaining personal hygiene and grooming under such conditions. Long, thick matted hair was commonplace, as were luxuriant beards that covered the face almost to the eyes and drooped far down upon the chest. Bay men looked "more like beasts than men, with the hairy clothing we wear," said James Isham, long-time factor at York Factory. And they smelled like bears: Soap was a luxury rarely seen at an HBC outpost, and the cold made thorough cleansing difficult in any event.

An early-19th-century engraving of the interior of a Cree Indian tent. The Cree were the "near Indians" with whom the HBC men conducted most of their trade. Each spring, after the breakup of the winter ice, the Cree would bring their heavily laden canoes to the HBC outposts to trade. The Cree also acted as middlemen in an exchange network that linked the HBC with "far Indians" such as the Blackfoot and the Assiniboin.

Summertime brought different torments, chief among them Hudson Bay's legendary insect infestations. Temperatures that reached as high as 80°F were accompanied by swarms of mosquitoes and sand flies so thick as to merit comparison with a biblical plague. James Knight, who spent more than 25 years with the company at a variety of stations, described one typical onslaught in 1717:

> Here is now such swarms of small sand flyes that wee can hardly see the sun through them and where they light is just as if a spark of fire fell and raises a little bump which smarts and burns so that we cannot forbear rubbing of them as it causes such scabbs that our hands and faces is nothing but scabbs. They fly into our ears nose eyes mouth and down our throat as we be most sorely plagued with them.

The only remedy available to the Bay men was to string mosquito netting above where they slept, a solution that most rejected as unmanly. Flooding caused by the spring breakup of the ice was another regular warm-weather bedevilment, as were, for the masters of the incoming supply ships from London, the various floes that broke away from the shore ice and cruised the bay all summer long and the icebergs that guarded the bay's entrance year-round.

The consolations for such a life were few. Food was one—the Bay men ate exceptionally well, as a result of both the rich store of provisions brought them each year by the supply ships and the abundance of game animals, fish, and birds that lived in the region—but chief among them was alcohol, which was imbibed in prodigious quantity despite official company policy, set in London, discouraging its use. Because of their low alcohol content, beer and wine froze very easily, making rum and "brandy" the beverages of choice. The Bay men loved real French brandy, but it was expensive and difficult to obtain; in its absence, they contented themselves with their own variation. "English brandy" was nothing more than raw gin colored with iodine or molasses. Consumed in huge quantities at the posts, it was soon to become a staple of trade with the Indians. Other home concoctions included spruce beer, the recipe for which called for firing gunpowder into the brew; and bumbo, a mixture of rum, water, sugar, and nutmeg. Accidents resulting from the drunkenness of Bay men, especially fires and drownings, were not uncommon, and more than one man used alcohol to permanently lift the loneliness and isolation that defined life at an HBC outpost. Suicide, aided and abetted by drink, was common enough to be known as "brandy death."

The companionship of Indian women was an equally commonplace and less destructive (at least from the Bay men's perspective) means of easing the harshness of the long winter. Although officially discouraged by HBC directive until the 19th century, long-term "marriages" between Bay men and Indian women occurred frequently, short-term sexual liaisons more often still. Such marriages were more than just a matter of sexual convenience for the traders; they were often encouraged by both Indians and HBC men in the field as a means of furthering relations between the two cultures. The Indian women and their relatives gained a certain level of material comfort and year-round access to the fort and its trading network; the traders gained an interpreter and an instructor in the ways of her tribe as well as a companion and helpmate. The marriages often had a political component; matches were made between the daughter of a prominent Indian— often the so-called trading chief or trading captain who spoke for his people in conducting the actual bartering— and the chief factor as a formal recognition of the bond that existed between the traders and the Indians. It was this aspect of the Indian-white liaisons that HBC governor George Simpson at last openly acknowledged in 1821:

> Connubial alliances are the best security we can have of the good will of the natives. I have therefore recommended the Gentlemen to form connections with the principal [Indian] Families immediately upon their arrival, which is no difficult matter, as the offer of their Wives and Daughters is the first token of their friendship and hospitality.

Indeed, the best traders were usually veteran Bay men who had entered into long-term marriages with an Indian woman.

As can be inferred from Simpson's directive, however, sexual relationships between whites and Indians were often exploitative. Many such unions were or became genuine love matches, but in numerous cases the women involved were treated as little more than property, sold to traders for guns and horses with small regard for their own wishes or feelings. Few marriages lasted longer than the Bay man's term of contract; most husbands vanished aboard the supply ships when their tour of duty ended. Prostitution thrived at many of the outposts, and the Blackfoot, the

Cree, and the Assiniboin all sold women taken captive in war to the HBC traders.

The various hardships and inequities of life at the outposts of the Hudson's Bay Company concerned its London officers only to the extent that they affected profits. Managerial and fiscal conservatism and an impenetrable corporate secrecy were the company's hallmarks, so long as its system worked, and for decades it worked exceptionally well. Each June or July the flotilla of Indian canoes, overloaded with furs, arrived at the trading posts; elaborate formal ceremonies were held, with eloquent oratory and the smoking of the peace pipe; and goods were bartered for furs. Every September the big ships from London anchored in the bay, the coming year's supplies were unloaded and taken ashore, the pelts and skins were stored in the ship's hold for the voyage back to England, and the Bay men settled in for another long winter.

The lay of the land beyond Hudson Bay remained a mystery, but the London officers and the Bay men alike were united in their lack of curiosity. They knew about it all that they needed to know—that from somewhere in the interior the Indians brought them their furs. Any other knowledge was irrelevant, and it would remain so for the

Peter Rindisbacher's drawing of a Cree Indian family on its way to trade at York Factory. Rindisbacher was a Swiss immigrant who as a 15-year-old in 1821 was among the settlers of the Red River Colony, the first permanent settlement, outside of fur-trading outposts, in the Canadian West.

Hudson's Bay Company as long as the Indians came to them. The company actually did all that it could to discourage further exploration, for it wanted nothing to upset its profitable system, particularly discoveries that might tend to encourage settlement or another method of trade. (Settlement was generally bad for business. The Indians tolerated and even welcomed fur traders, whose interests lay in maintaining the wilderness as wilderness and in preserving harmonious working relations with them. The same could not be said of settlers, who claimed the land as their own and regarded its native inhabitants as intruders to be killed or driven off.) This approach earned the Hudson's Bay Company much criticism for its lack of initiative—"The Company have for eighty years slept at the edge of a frozen sea; they have shown no curiosity to penetrate farther themselves, and have exerted all their art and power to crush that spirit in others," wrote Joseph Robson, a Bay man who became a vociferous critic of the HBC—but the directors stolidly shrugged it off and conducted business as usual.

The HBC's few desultory inland forays—the most significant of them Henry Kelsey's exploration of the Saskatchewan River in 1690–92, in the course of which he became the first white man to see the Canadian prairie—were conducted for strictly business purposes, and their results were known only to the company's officers. Kelsey's motivation, for example, was not exploration but "to call, encourage and invite the remoter Indians"—the Salteaux, the Assiniboin, and the Blackfoot—to bring their furs to the bay to trade. His journey can hardly be said to have added immediately to the store of available geographic information about the Canadian West, because for the most part it was kept secret. According to the historian Glyndwr Williams, "What, if anything, the company made of Kelsey's journey is totally obscure. It failed to use, publish or even preserve the notes of his findings. No evidence of his wanderings appear on contemporary maps; the episode was an isolated and soon-forgotten feat in an era when Company servants were reluctant to move away from the bayside posts." As HBC profits doubled during the two years of Kelsey's expedition, there seemed little need for the company to concern itself with his discoveries or the rest of the interior. The same treatment was generally accorded the voyages of the ships occasionally sent, in response to criticism of the company's inertia, to the western head of the bay in halfhearted search of a northwest passage.

By the midpoint of the 18th century, however, this was changing, as the Hudson's Bay Company found itself gradually being outflanked to the south and west by first French Canadian and later Scottish merchant-adventurers willing to travel into the interior to bring their goods directly to the Indians—or at least closer to them than the Bay men were willing to come. The most important of these was the fur trader Pierre Gaultier de Varennes, Sieur de La Vérendrye, who with the aid of his three sons established seven fortified trading posts to the northwest of Lake Superior, in the vicinity of Lake Winnipeg and the Red, Assiniboin, and Winnipeg rivers, in the 1730s and 1740s. As Mackenzie later put it, there was not a "finer country in the world for the residence of uncivilized man," not to mention beavers, and the pedlars who followed in La Vérendrye's footsteps (and ventured even farther west) profited accordingly.

The Hudson's Bay Company immediately felt the effects of this competition. In 1732, by which time La Vérendrye had completed his first two trading posts, the number of beaver skins taken in trade at York Factory dropped 15 percent from the previous year's harvest. As York then took in about half of the company's annual yield in furs, the decline was significant, and it continued in succeeding years.

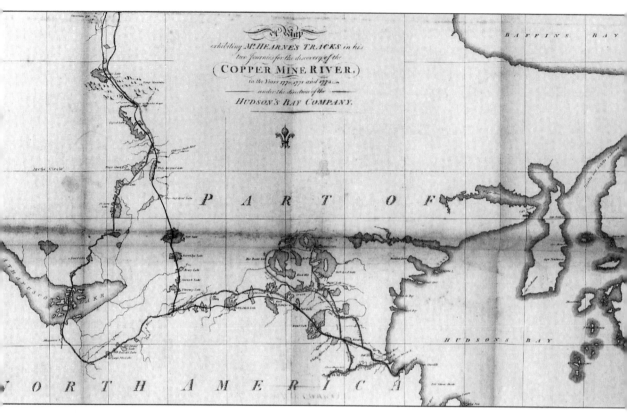

This map appeared opposite the title page of Samuel Hearne's account of his travels in the Canadian North, which eventually took him from Prince of Wales's Fort along the Coppermine River to the Arctic Ocean. Hearne was a keen and unbiased observer of both the landscape and the ways of the Indians he encountered on his arduous treks.

The advent of the pedlars therefore forced the Hudson's Bay Company to adopt a number of new strategies. Alcohol was now made more freely available to the Indians. Previously, the Bay men, though often enthusiastic imbibers themselves, had severely restricted, if not quite outrightly prohibited, its distribution among the Indians. The earlier policy resulted more from a concern with profits than with alcohol's deleterious effects on Indian culture: Drunken Indians, as the Bay men saw it, were less productive trappers, and they could be dangerous and unpredictable as well. The pedlars had fewer compunctions on this score, and as the Indians soon grew to expect alcohol as a trade item, the Bay men believed they had little choice but to supply what the Indians demanded. Even so, they often found themselves at a disadvantage in this regard to the French Canadian traders, whose brandy was far superior to their own version and to the rum the English imported from the Caribbean.

The Hudson's Bay Company did have several trade advantages that it was able to successfully exploit, however. The more highly developed state of Britain's manufacturing industries, in comparison with France's, meant the HBC's metal and cloth goods were generally of higher quality and cost less than those sold by French Canadian traders. At midcentury, a gun at an HBC outpost would cost an Indian 14 beaver skins; a similar weapon bought from a pedlar would set the trapper back 20 pelts. One of the famous and highly desired HBC blankets, with its colored stripes indicating its worth, sold for 7 skins, whereas the inferior wraps sold by the pedlars cost 10. The single greatest advantage owned by the Hudson's Bay Company was the superiority of its tobacco, which the Indians coveted almost as much as spirits. Imported from Brazil, the English variety was a smooth and pleasing blend; its French counterpart was said to taste like sawdust.

Its newfound willingness to traffic in intoxicants and its superior goods were not alone sufficient for the Hudson's Bay Company to maintain its trade advantage, however, and as a result even its conservative management was in time forced to authorize several exploratory ventures with an eye toward the possible establishment of posts away from the bay. In 1754, an HBC net mender named Anthony Henday was sent west from York House to "draw down many of the Indians to trade." Accompanied by several Cree Indians, he traveled west on the Saskatchewan River and its north fork to within 40 miles of the Rocky Mountains. Curiously, he made no mention of the great range in his journal; his attention seems to have been more closely drawn by the French Canadian traders he seemed to encounter everywhere, from their outpost at the Saskatchewan's headwaters to the Indian villages located near the site of the present-day city of Edmonton. "I don't like it," he confided in his journal, although he acknowledged their greater initiative and drive. "The French talk several [Indian] languages to perfection; they have the advantage of us in every shape, and if they had Brazil tobacco would entirely cut our trade off." Moses Cocking, an HBC bookkeeper sent on a similar westward reconnaissance in the early 1770s, reached the same conclusion: The pedlars were firmly established on the Saskatchewan and were doing great harm to the HBC trade. The books at York Factory told the same story. In 1773, the factory took in only 8,000 beaver skins. Just a few decades earlier, the average annual yield was more than 30,000.

Reluctantly, the company decided to move into the interior. In 1774, Samuel Hearne established Cumberland House, the first permanent HBC outpost away from the shores of Hudson Bay, at Cumberland Lake, about 450 miles southwest of York Factory. Hearne was the most remarkable of the HBC explorers. Originally a sailor aboard HBC supply ships rather than a true Bay man, in three overland expeditions undertaken in the years 1769–71 he walked from Prince of Wales's Fort (also

Hearne's drawing of Prince of Wales's Fort, the HBC outpost near the mouth of the Churchill River that was the starting point for his expeditions to the Arctic. With its 40 cannons, Prince of Wales's Fort, which took 40 years to build, was the most secure of the HBC outposts.

known as Churchill Factory) northwest across the marshy barrens—with their dwarf spruce, scrub pine, abundant waterfowl, and herds of musk-oxen and caribou—and tundra of northwest Canada all the way to the mouth of the Coppermine River, where it enters the Arctic Ocean in Coronation Gulf. In the more than 200 years since, only a half-dozen men have duplicated his trek, yet it won Hearne little credit with his employers, for the Coppermine proved to be neither a viable northwest passage nor to have rich mineral deposits along its shores.

Hearne's establishment of Cumberland House proved to be a better means of winning his superiors' gratitude, especially when he arrived at York Factory in the summer of 1775 at the head of a flotilla of 32 Indian canoes, all of them loaded with furs. He pronounced himself eager to establish HBC outposts even farther westward but was rewarded instead, at the young age of 30, with the position of chief factor at Prince of Wales's Fort. One interior trading post would be sufficient for now, the London officers decreed, little aware that they were yet to face their greatest challenge.

Lake Athabasca in wintertime, as drawn by Hearne. The Nor'Westers' exploitation of the Athabasca region would temporarily end the HBC domination of the fur trade.

The Nor'Westers

The joining together of the most enterprising pedlars to form the amalgamation known as the North West Company constituted the most formidable challenge ever faced by the Hudson's Bay Company. From their company's beginnings, the Nor'Westers' approach to the fur business stood in sharp contrast to the Bay men's stodgier methods. Regarding unexplored territory as an affront, the Nor'Westers ventured ever farther into the Canadian interior until within a few short years of the company's founding, through the vision of Pond and the ambition of Mackenzie, they were contemplating reaching the Pacific itself. This breadth of vision made the North West Company, in the words of Peter C. Newman, the "first North American business to operate on a continental scale." Connected by a navy of 2,000 canoeists, who plied the numerous lakes and rivers that are just one of Canada's myriad natural blessings, its network of offices and outposts stretched, in the spring of 1788, as Mackenzie was making his way to the summer meeting at Grand Portage, more than 4,000 miles, from Montreal to Athabasca. And if Mackenzie was able to prove Pond right, that network would soon be extended to the Pacific, giving the western outposts easy access to deep-sea shipping.

The Nor'Westers conducted themselves with a swagger and flair seldom seen in their counterparts from Hudson Bay, where a strict hierarchy, with limited prospects of

Pedlars entice the Indians to trade. By establishing themselves nearer to where the Indians lived than did the HBC men, the Nor'Westers were able to wrest the most lucrative portion of the fur trade away from the Hudson's Bay Company.

upward mobility and a military-style formality and discipline, prevailed. In large part, this élan was attributable to the fact that each of the major NWC officers in the field were also partners in the company, whereas even the highest-ranking Bay man was never more than a paid employee. The Nor'Westers' ebullience also derived from the flush of newfound success and wealth. Within 20 years of its founding, the North West Company controlled 78 percent of the Canadian fur trade, and its partners had increased the worth of their original investment by more than 200 percent. Annual dividends on a single share of stock averaged £400—4 times the yearly salary of a clerk at an HBC outpost.

Whereas the HBC directors kept close guard over the company's ledgers and coffers, the NWC partners flaunted their wealth, often in spectacular fashion. Most Bay men returned to England as soon as they could (the HBC's profits flowed to London as well), but the Nor'Westers, for the most part, set down New World roots. The wealthiest Montreal partners built fabulous houses at the foot of the city's Mount Royal, and NWC earnings made the Bank of Montreal, for a time, North America's most powerful financial institution. The 19th-century American writer Washington Irving, author of one of the first histories of the fur trade, wrote of the "gorgeous prodigality" of the NWC partners. "Sometimes one or two partners, recently

The city of Montreal as it appeared near the end of the 18th century. The success of the North West Company and other fur-trading concerns brought it great prosperity at that time.

from the interior posts, would make their appearance in New York," wrote Irving. "On these occasions there was a degree of magnificence of the purse about them, and a peculiar propensity to expenditure at the goldsmiths and jeweller's for rings, chains, brooches, necklaces, jewelled watches, and other rich trinkets, partly for their own wear, partly for presents to their female acquaintances."

During their Montreal sojourns, these lords of the wilderness were known for their high-spirited hijinks. One wintering partner always shod his horse with silver horseshoes and delighted in galloping masked through the city's poorer neighborhoods, scattering coins among the urchins and beggars. This same individual often rode his mount right into the dining rooms of Montreal's poshest restaurants, demanded a place be set for it, and ordered it a five-star meal.

But the most boisterous antics took place at the NWC's own supper club—the Beaver Club, the most exclusive fraternal organization on the continent. Membership was limited to 55 traders who had spent a full season in le pays d'en haut, a requirement that eliminated even Simon McTavish, who had never wintered in the north country. Upon admission to the Beaver Club, a new member received a gold medal, engraved with his name and the date of his first winter in the north. On one side of the medal appeared a likeness of the fur-bearing, bucktoothed rodent that inspired the energy and enterprise displayed by the Nor'Westers, along with the company motto, Industry & Perseverance; on the other, an image of a canoe, conducted by four voyageurs, and the club motto, Fortitude in Distress.

The medal had to be worn to the fortnightly meetings of the Beaver Club, which were always held at one of Montreal's finest dining establishments. Supper was served at four in the afternoon; it consisted of such wilderness delicacies as venison steaks, pemmican wedges, roasted beaver tails, and pickled buffalo tongues and was punctuated by the five mandatory toasts—to the mother of all saints; to the king; to the fur trade in all its branches; to voyageurs, wives, and children; and to absent members. The toasts had to be given in precisely the order listed; any deviation subjected a member to a fine of six bottles of wine. After each toast, each member fired his glass into the dining room fireplace; after the final salutation, an Indian peace pipe was passed around, and supper was concluded.

At that point, many of the Beaver Club's married men and less boisterous members called it a night, but several always stayed on to reminisce of the old days in the north country, and it was a rare club meeting that ever broke up before dawn. Surviving accounts of typical Beaver Club gatherings describe the members dancing on tables among the china, crockery, and wine and liquor bottles, falling to the floor and injuring themselves, and singing endless voyageur songs. An early-morning highlight of each meeting was the re-creation of the canoe voyage north: The members sat on the floor, two abreast, clutching swords, bellows, and any other implements that could be made to serve as "paddles," and piloted their imaginary canoe on its way. To "run the rapids," they clambered up on top of the much-abused dining tables and "shot" to the floor astride empty wine kegs. Many limbs and skulls were broken in the process; by dawn, according to Newman, the "rented dining room resembled the field hospital of a vanquished army."

At such revels, even Mackenzie dropped his usually impenetrable reserve. Participants report him whooping and singing with the best of the members. A guest at one such gathering, watching stuporously from the fireplace— "By six or seven o'clock, I had, in common with many of the others, fallen from my seat. To save my legs from being trampled on, I drew myself into the fireplace, and sat up in one of the corners. . . . I there remained very passive"—observed Mackenzie and his friend William

(continued on page 50)

Hats and Dams

The animal that inspired so much energy and enterprise on the part of the Nor'Westers, their counterparts on Hudson Bay, and the many Indian tribes with whom they traded was a large buck-toothed aquatic rodent—*Castor fiber* according to scientific classification—with thick brown fur, webbed feet, a broad, flat tail, and squinty eyes. Worth more than gold to the fur traders and Indians that hunted it, the beaver thrived in unsettled North America, with its seemingly unending forests and countless waterways.

For the Indians, the beaver had long been an object of respect, if not veneration, an integral part of their environment, and a major character in much of their mythology. According to the Ojibwa, the Great Spirit sent the beaver to dive beneath the waters that then covered the earth. Using its tail as a shovel, the beaver dredged up mud from the water's bottom and created the lands of earth. The Algonquin believed that thunder was caused by the booming slap of a beaver's tail on the water. Many tribes believed that beavers had once been able to speak, but because they exhibited so much intelligence and so many other fine qualities, the Great Spirit took away their power of speech so that they would not become superior to humans.

Later, after they began bartering its pelt for trade goods, the Indians had other reasons to admire the beaver. "The beaver does everything well. He makes us kettles, axes, swords, knives and gives us drink and food without the trouble of cultivating the ground," said a Montagnais Indian.

Beavers truly are remarkable creatures. It has been said that aside from humans, they are the only animals able to fashion their own environments for living. Using its four sharp front incisors to gnaw with, a beaver can fell a tree six inches in diameter in five minutes. The beaver gnaws on wood continually, as a matter of dual necessity. The branches from felled trees are used to build the huge, intricate lodges beavers live in and the dams they erect upstream to control waterflow to their abodes. Their constant lumberjacking also serves to keep their front teeth honed down. If not worn by constant use, the incisors can grow up to seven inches long and would eventually pierce the animal's skull.

Beaver lodges are made of tree branches, logs, and mud. The beaver makes the foundation for its home by anchoring twigs in a river or lake bottom with stones and mud. Intertwined tree branches and trunks, insulated with tufts of grass, serve as the lodges' outer walls, which are then plastered with mud. During winter, the mud freezes, making the lodges impregnable to all intruders. The beaver secretes enough birch, willow, and poplar sprigs inside for its family to feed on during the winter, and the lodge is riddled with breathing chimneys and emergency exits. Somehow, the animal is able to anticipate at what level the water around its home will freeze during the winter, and its living den within the lodge, where it sleeps on mats made of twigs and grass, is always located above the freezing line.

Upstream from its living quarters, the beaver constructs massive dams—some as large as 1 mile in length, 40 feet in width, and containing 250 tons of building material—that control the flow of water to its lodge. The first settlers of North America were astonished by the complexity of the beaver's constructions. Some reported that beavers lived in three-story "castles" complete with balconies, moats, and living rooms. Although the truth is somewhat less glamorous, the beaver's capacity as an engineer has continued to fascinate and baffle naturalists.

Traders and European dandies were more taken with the beaver's thick fur than with its building prowess. From the 16th to the mid-19th century in Europe, a beaver hat was the single most desirable item of fashionable apparel for men and women, worn by everyone from soldiers to clergymen. Intricate rules of etiquette governed the donning and doffing of a beaver, and its style and quality spoke volumes about its wearer's social and economic status. According to the historian Walter O'Meara, "To own a fine beaver was to prove one a man—or woman—of the beau monde. To appear without one was to be quite hopelessly out of style." This fashion created an insatiable demand for beaver skins, for, as O'Meara points out, "There was only one kind of fur out of which a beaver hat could be made, and that, quite naturally, was the beaver's."

A 17th-century illustration of a beaver.

The medal presented to worthy fur traders upon their admission to the Beaver Club. This medal belonged to James McGill, whose fortune, earned in part from the fur trade, founded McGill University.

(continued from page 47)

McGillivray (who would ultimately succeed McTavish as the head of the NWC) teetering on the edge of consciousness. As Mackenzie was attempting to push a bottle of spirits across the table to McGillivray so that the two traders could drink a last toast to the brave comrades fallen around them, "he slid off his chair, and could not recover his seat." A similar mishap befell McGillivray as he reached for the bottle. And so—with its greatest explorer asleep on the floor with its future chief and other less-notables—ended another gathering of the bold men of the North West Company.

But such outrageous conduct represented the Nor'Westers at play; it was their workaday life that made them truly remarkable. Their rapid rise to preeminence in the fur trade was made possible by their application of the company motto, Perseverance; by their willingness to push their outposts to anywhere there were beaver skins to be had; and by their mastery of the lakes and rivers that collectively constituted the inland waterway that connected the two ends of their empire.

The transportation system that linked Montreal with Athabasca and the other western outposts was the single most critical aspect of the NWC operation. Each spring, as soon as the ice began to break up, usually at the beginning of May, the Montreal-based voyageurs, known as *les allants et vallants* (the goers and comers), hiked the nine-mile road from Montreal to above the St. Lawrence's unnavigable Lachine Rapids, where the NWC staging ground was located. There, the Montreal *bourgeois*, as the NWC commanding officers were known, supervised the loading of the large—36 to 40 feet long and 5 feet wide—*canots de maître* (freight canoes). Made, Indian fashion, by stitching a birch-bark skin around a cedar frame with tree roots and then caulking the seams with resinous gum or pine pitch, these remarkable vessels could carry four tons of crew and freight. They constituted as well one of the NWC's few technological advantages in its competition with the HBC. As birch bark is exceptional in its resistance to dampness and extremes of temperature and its strength and pliability, and birch trees did not grow around Hudson Bay, the HBC boats were inferior to the NWC models.

When the canoes—known as birchbarks—were fully loaded, their gunwales just six inches above the water level, the NWC flotilla, which usually consisted of several brigades of 4 to 10 canoes apiece, set off. The voyageurs followed west and south from Montreal the river route to the Great Lakes pioneered by Samuel de Champlain in the first decade of the 17th century: upriver a short distance on the St. Lawrence, then west on the Ottawa River to Lake Nipissing, south on the French River to the Georgian Bay of Lake Huron, and westward through the straits of Sault Ste. Marie into Lake Superior, on whose western shore stood Grand Portage, the frontier headquarters of the North West Company. Completed in seven or eight weeks, punctuated by backbreaking portages and stretches of rapids, it was a journey much more easily summarized than made.

Its successful completion each year was attributable to the tirelessness and the skill of the North West Company's 1,100 voyageurs, the boatmen—nearly all of them French Canadian—responsible for manning the NWC canoes. Most were the younger sons of farming families from the villages along the St. Lawrence Valley. Bearing recommendations from their parish priest, they signed on with the NWC for terms of up to 3 years, for which they were given an annual salary of £25 to £50 a year and certain essentials—a pair of trousers, a couple of shirts, a blanket, moccasins, and several pounds of tobacco. In exchange, they were responsible for transporting the company's goods, fur, and personnel between Montreal, Grand Portage, and the western outposts.

The self-styled elite of the NWC voyageur corps were *les hommes du nord* (the men of the north), who plied the waterways between the western posts and Grand Portage and wintered in the north country, where they earned their keep by driving dogsleds—a skill learned from the Indians—between outposts to deliver messages and supplies. The men of the north looked down on their eastern counterparts, the goers and comers. A similar pecking order prevailed within the boats themselves. The lowest-ranking voyageurs were the *milieux*, who squatted two abreast in the middle of the canoes and paddled—the usual rate was 45 strokes a minute—according to the orders given them by the *avant* (bowsman) or the *gouvernail* (steersman). Each brigade of canoes came under the overall direction of a guide, the highest position a voyageur could hope to attain. The guides were responsible for daily travel schedules and the safety of the cargo being transported. They were paid three times the salary of the milieux and were accorded the signal honor of being allowed to eat with the bourgeois at Grand Portage. On the river, they were allowed to sleep in tents; the other voyageurs took shelter under an overturned canoe.

The skill of these "natural water dogs," as an envious HBC trader referred to them, is attested to by the fact that the NWC suffered an annual average loss of less than one percent of cargo carried. The voyageurs' esprit de corps and stamina became legendary, as did their colorful appearance. The voyageurs paddled from dawn to sundown, crooning their alternately salacious and tender chanteys and ballads most of that time (although singing was forbidden before the eight o'clock stop for breakfast), with five minutes allotted every hour for them to light their ever-present pipes. (Distances were accordingly measured in pipes, not miles or hours.) This backbreaking schedule was maintained on an unvarying daily diet of about a pound and a half of pemmican—dried buffalo meat and berries mixed with fat—if one were un homme du nord, and a thick mush of fatty pork, peas, and cornmeal for the comers and goers. (*Mangeur du lard* [pork eater] was regarded as a supreme insult by the men of the north, whose greatest boast was likewise "Je suis [I am] un homme du nord.") Unlike the American fur traders, who hunted for their food on their way west, the voyageurs had no spare time to waste in search of game if they were to reach their destination and return during the short summer season. This monotonous diet, which was nevertheless fairly high in nutritional value, was sometimes supplemented by *galette*, a kind of bread cooked as flat cakes on a griddle.

The voyageurs wore buckskin coats or *capots* (hooded frock coats with brass buttons) over red-and-black flannel shirts, corduroy pants cinched at the waist with crimson sashes, and deerskin moccasins without socks. This colorful ensemble was topped off with a varying selection of headgear—bright handkerchiefs wrapped as turbans, wool tuques, or tasseled nightcaps. These "hats" were often decorated with feathers or even the tail of a fox. Most wore their hair very long—to their shoulders or below—to protect their necks from insects; likewise, by shaking his head, a voyageur could use his hair as a horse did its tail, to shoo away mosquitoes and gnats. Their boats and equipment were similarly adorned. The canoes were usually

Voyageurs transport a bourgeois and his wife. For all the hardship of their life, the voyageurs seemed to one contemporary observer to be the "happiest people in existence."

painted with the "N. W. Co." insignia and other designs, such as a stallion rearing or the head of an Indian chief in war dress. The voyageurs stained their cedar paddles blue or green and then added designs in black or red.

Voyageurs had to be phenomenally strong but not overly big, for most of the room in a canoe had to be reserved for cargo and long legs did not easily fit in among the vessel's thwarts. Most were relatively short, wiry fellows with powerful, deep chests, strong shoulders, and highly developed arm muscles. Few were taller than five feet six inches, and the optimum height was a couple of inches shorter than that.

Just short of Grand Portage, the Montreal brigades put in to shore to prepare for the grand entrance. Each voyageur donned a red tasseled cap and a blue coat; the bourgeois put on tall top hats made of beaver skin. The company flag was raised in the prow, and the brigades of canoes swept down into the harbor, their crews shouting and singing.

At Grand Portage, which consisted of 16 wooden buildings, including warehouses, a stone magazine, some stores, living quarters, and a dining hall, surrounded by a 15-foot-high cedar palisade, these "natural water dogs" became beasts of burden. The trade goods brought from Montreal by the comers and goers had to be transferred to a depot at Pigeon River, from where they would be carried west by the men of the north. This was the grand portage from which the NWC headquarters received its name—a nine-mile trail across rocky hills and muddy, flat ground. Each voyageur was required to take 2 of the 90-pound sacks in which the North West Company packaged its trade goods (each sack was called a *piece*) on his back and, after fastening them to himself by means of leather lines wrapped around his forehead, carry them over the portage to Pigeon River. Such a load outweighed the average voyageur, who generally tipped the scales at about 150 pounds; nevertheless, many earned the bonus of a

Spanish peso offered for carrying a third piece, and some, in order to win a wager or simply to flaunt their machismo, were known to carry 4 pieces at once. The record of five pieces on a single trip was held by a strongman named Pierre Bonga, who was exceptional for more than his herculean strength: Bonga was a black man from the West Indies. Although the portage was divided into 16 *poses*, or rest stops, the voyageurs still said that it was easier to get to heaven than to Pigeon River. Each of the Montreal men was expected to make four crossings—a total of eight pieces—of the grand portage.

His portages completed, a voyageur had some time to play. Except on special occasions, voyageurs, like Indians, were not allowed inside the walls of the fort. They accordingly spent most of their time carousing outside the stockade walls at the *cantine salope*, where for a price one could buy liquor, a meal, or the companionship of a young lady, most of them mixed-blood Chippewa or Cree girls. Brawling and knife fights, especially between the men of the north and the "pork eaters," were commonplace. Those voyageurs who got too out of hand were confined for days at a time in the *pot au beurre* (butter tub)—a wooden privy.

The one occasion on which the voyageurs were allowed inside the fort was the annual ball, the high point of every summer season at Grand Portage. On that evening, the Great Hall was laid out for a banquet. Long tables, groaning under the weight of huge platters of beef and venison, smoked hams, roast potatoes, and baked whitefish, stretched its length, and hundreds of candles flickered inside. Simon McTavish and the other partners sat at the table of honor in front of the tremendous fireplace; all were decked out in silk vests and gray coats, with their dress swords affixed at their side. While eating heartily—the meal was prepared by cooks brought from Montreal especially for that purpose—and quaffing rum, port, or madeira, the partners offered frequent toasts, including the five man-

A trader proffers his wares. Although the fur trade's long-term effects were destructive to Indian culture, for the most part the Indians participated in the trade as willing partners, bartering something that was of no inherent value to them—beaver skins—for items that they valued greatly, such as metal tools and weapons.

datory salutations of the Beaver Club. When the dining was over, the tables were pushed back against the walls, the Great Hall's doors were opened wide, and the voyageurs—dressed in their best finery—and the Indians were admitted. Dancing, to the sound of bagpipes, flutes, and violins, commenced with McTavish taking the floor with the daughter of a local chief. The music and frivolity usually continued until sunrise.

Although Mackenzie sometimes complained of the boredom and isolation that was an unavoidable part of much of the fur trade, and he could be downright disdainful of the way of life it entailed and the company it forced a man to keep—"I think it unpardonable in any man to remain in this country who can afford to leave it," he would write to his cousin Roderick McKenzie—he could be as rugged as any voyageur and was no stranger to the various wilderness indulgences with which the Nor'Westers consoled themselves. His occasional monumental revels at the Beaver Club apparently dissipated little of the legendary stamina that allowed him to once snowshoe 700 miles to attend a Christmas dinner and paddle 72 miles on a day so frigid that his voyageurs, but not himself, resorted to fingerless mittens. Exceptionally handsome, he also enjoyed several "open-air marriages" and fathered at least two children—Maria and Andrew—by Indian mothers.

In the summer of 1788 at Grand Portage, Mackenzie was preoccupied by what he had learned from Pond and with his proposal to attempt a western voyage to the ocean. His enthusiasm persuaded the NWC senior partners to approve his venture, and as soon as the smaller *canots du nord* (canoes of the north measured just 24 feet in length and 4 feet across at the beam and were manned by only 6 voyageurs) were loaded, he set out for Fort Chipewyan, a new NWC outpost that Roderick McKenzie was constructing on the south shore of Lake Athabasca. (Among the unusual touches that Roderick insisted upon for Fort Chipewyan was a library of books imported from England; their number eventually grew so large that a separate building had to be erected to accommodate them. Fort Chipewyan was also the only NWC post that was painted on the inside. Such touches made it an outpost of culture and refinement in the lonely West, and it was soon dubbed Little Athens by the Nor'Westers.)

Mackenzie was apparently able to communicate his excitement to his voyageurs, for they made the journey from Grand Portage to Athabasca, via the Pigeon River, Rainy

Roderick McKenzie, a cousin of Alexander Mackenzie's, oversaw the construction of Fort Chipewyan. The "Little Athens" of the fur trade was originally situated on the south shore of Lake Athabasca; later, it was relocated north of the lake.

Alcohol abuse often reduced the Indians to ragged poverty. According to Ogden Tanner, a white American who lived among the Canadian Indians for many years, the "alienation of mind produced by liquor" often caused them to commit suicide.

Lake, Lake of the Woods, the Winnipeg River, Lake Winnipeg, the Saskatchewan River, Lac La Ronge, the Churchill River, the Clearwater, and various portages, in a record 52 days—more than 2 weeks shorter than usual. Probably he appealed to their competitive spirit in order to get more speed out of them. As the northernmost of the men of the north, the Athabascans considered themselves the elite of the elite, and they were always willing to race another brigade or enter into a time trial to prove their superiority. Stops would in all likelihood have been made at the NWC pemmican stations at the mouth of the Winnipeg River and at Cumberland House on the Saskatchewan. (Cumberland House was actually an HBC outpost; the NWC depot, which went by the same name, was beside it.) Pemmican was brought to these stations by the Indians from the plains around the Assiniboin and Red rivers—areas rich in buffalo—and was traded for the usual variety of trade goods. There, it was packaged in the NWC's all-purpose 90-pound bags and stored for use by the voyageurs.

If there was a newcomer to the North among Mackenzie's party in 1788, another stop would have been made at or near the Methy Portage, the geographic dividing line between the Hudson Bay and Arctic river systems. There, the neophyte would be made to kneel in the canoe while a guide "baptized" him with a cedar sprig dipped in the waters of the northerly stream. At that point, the newly anointed northman would swear that he would never allow another new man to pass this point without performing a similar ceremony and that he would never kiss a fellow voyageur's wife without her permission. After the requisite celebratory toast, the newcomer was entitled to boast, for the first time, "Je suis un homme du nord."

Shortly afterward, the Athabasca brigades would arrive at Fort Chipewyan, where a scaled-down version of the events at Grand Portage, down to the fancy dress ball, would take place. Soon, the Indians arrived to be outfitted for their winter's trapping, on credit, with a gun, powder, shot, and traps. The Indians' debts were reckoned in terms of made-beaver skins, or *plus* (pronounced "plews")—a prime skin from an adult beaver. A gun at an NWC outpost cost 14 plus; a blanket, 6 plus; an ax or a trap, 2 plus. (Made-beavers were the basic item of currency at both NWC and HBC outposts; even the worth of furs from other animals was reckoned in terms of made-beavers.)

The highest-priced item, at 30 plus, was a 9-gallon keg of "high wine"—132-proof rum diluted with water at a ratio of 3 or 4 to 1 for veteran drinkers such as the Assiniboin and the Cree and 8 or 9 to 1 for less experienced topers such as the Blackfoot. (The latter concoction was known as Blackfoot rum.) Unlike their HBC counterparts, the Nor'Westers tended to believe that alcohol spurred, rather than hindered, Indian productivity in trapping. According to Duncan McGillivray, NWC partner and McTavish's nephew, "The love of rum is their first inducement to industry, they undergo every hardship and fatigue to procure a Skinfull of this delicious beverage, and when a Nation becomes addicted to drinking, it affords a strong presumption that they will soon become excellent hunters."

Once the Indians were equipped, it was time to settle in for the long winter. The voyageurs were kept busy running messages and supplies between outposts by dogsled. Their vehicles were decorated with bells and ribbons, and their dogs protected by heavy blankets and tiny deerskin boots for wear over jagged ice. For the partners, once the various accounts were reckoned and put in order, there was not that much to do, outside of the routine tasks necessary for survival. The monotony and boredom contributed to the sense of loneliness and isolation that often oppressed Mackenzie during the dark winter months. The winter of 1788–89 was more easily endured, however, for he knew that, come springtime, he would be heading for the Pacific.

River of Disappointment

With 12 companions, Alexander Mackenzie left Fort Chipewyan for what he believed would be a 200-mile journey westward to the Pacific Ocean on June 3, 1789. He returned 102 days later, on September 12, having traveled the length of Canada's longest river and back—a total of 2,060 miles—into a frosty wilderness never before visited by white men. That river—the Mackenzie—today bears the name of the first man to navigate its length, but its conqueror had a different name for it. He called it the River of Disappointment, for it yielded none of the secrets he had set out to reveal.

Of the 11 people who traveled with Mackenzie, the names of only 6 are known. There were 4 voyageurs—François Barrieu, Charles Ducette, Joseph Landry, and Pierre de Lorme—1 trader, John Steinbruck; and 6 Indians, 1 of whom was known as English Chief and had accompanied Samuel Hearne on his journey to the Coppermine River 18 years earlier. Two of the voyageurs brought their Indian wives along; two of the Indians were the wives of English Chief. The women served as guides and interpreters, as cooks, and as tailors and cobblers, making, mending, and repairing clothing and moccasins.

These 12 occupied 3 canoes; an NWC clerk named Laurent Leroux traveled with them temporarily in a separate canoe for the purpose of establishing a supply depot at Great Slave Lake. All four vessels were built of birch bark ribbed with white cedar and gummed with spruce

Roderick McKenzie was Alexander Mackenzie's frequent correspondent and closest friend. Introspective and bookish, McKenzie was something of an anomaly in the fur trade. While at Fort Chipewyan, McKenzie gathered a massive amount of information on the habits and customs of the local Indians, but he never wrote his proposed ethnological study.

Birch-bark canoes were the vessels with which Canada was explored. According to the historian Peter C. Newman, the North West Company used an "inland navy of two thousand canoeists" to challenge the Hudson's Bay Company. Seen here are drawings of canoes that accompanied the published journal of the Baron La Hontan, a 17th-century French explorer of the New World.

resin. The largest canoe had been designed by Mackenzie himself; it was 32 feet long, 4 feet 10 inches wide at the beam, 2 feet deep, weighed 300 pounds, and could carry up to 3,000 pounds of assorted trade goods, food, tents, blankets, and guns. Leroux's canoe was very similar; the

Indians paddled smaller craft. Cloths made waterproof by soaking them in corn oil and animal fat protected the loads from the elements at least part of the time. Mackenzie's boat also carried an oak mast and canvas sails for use in crossing the Great Slave Lake if the winds were favorable.

The bulk of the supplies carried by the explorers consisted of pemmican, packed in 90-pound portions in the NWC's distinctive rawhide bags. Although the group's diet was nowhere near as limited as that enjoyed by the voyageurs on the run to and from Grand Portage—the Indians, who had been hired as guides and hunters, brought in game almost daily, and Mackenzie's party often caught and ate fish—pemmican remained essential. (Into the 20th century, this long-lasting, easily packaged high-energy food remained a staple of overland expeditions of exploration. For example, in becoming, in 1911, the first to reach the South Pole, the Norwegian explorer Roald Amundsen and his men relied on a commercially manufactured variety of pemmican for sustenance.) Wild licorice root and a dozen varieties of berries provided additional variety and carbohydrates. Mackenzie's party, which was working 12 to 18 hours a day and sometimes traveled as much as 100 miles in a single day—a tremendous rate of progress over unexplored territory—ate ravenously. At one point, the 13 explorers consumed 2 entire "reindeer" (as Mackenzie called caribou), 4 swans, 46 geese, and innumerable fish over a span of just 6 days. Although the men ate more than the women, the average ration per person worked out to more than eight pounds of food per day.

Various legends about the unexplored areas to the north and west had long been circulated among the fur traders by the Indians with whom they did business. The most common were of incredibly fierce, warlike tribes, some of whom were said to engage in cannibalism. Other stories were told of raging whirlpools, impassable rapids, and strange, even monstrous, creatures. Although such tales were, at best, only partly rooted in truth, the Indians were not just being fanciful—their interests, of course, were not served by the fur traders advancing farther into the interior. Mackenzie, no doubt, had heard such reports, but his businesslike resolve did not allow him to speculate much on the possible dangers of the unknown.

In any event, the greatest challenges he and his party had to face initially were of a kind well known to the Nor'Westers—rough water and horrible weather. Their first day's travel, conducted in blustery, wet weather, took them across the west end of Lake Athabasca to the mouth of the Slave River. The next day, while fighting a biting northwest wind, the swift rapids between present-day Fort Fitzgerald and Fort Smith, along the border separating Alberta from the Northwest Territories (the western portion of which is known today as the District of Mackenzie), claimed one of their canoes and all its cargo. They proceeded more cautiously on the Slave afterward. Although most voyageurs preferred running even the most dangerous rapids to a portage, Mackenzie's party made six such overland detours en route to Great Slave Lake. Birchbarks could carry tremendous loads, but they were nevertheless extremely fragile and had to be delicately handled by the voyageurs. They were always carried ashore at night, never dragged, and most nights the voyageurs spent considerable time caulking joints and seams and making other repairs before they slid beneath their vessels to sleep.

Even though winter's darkness had given way to the long hours of daylight of the sub-Arctic summer—enabling Mackenzie to push his party from three in the morning to nine at night—snow fell often on the early days of the journey, and in the course of the four-hour nights the temperature sometimes fell so rapidly that Mackenzie woke in the morning to find the river frozen and his fish traps iced over. On June 9, they reached the Great Slave Lake, only to find much of its surface still covered with ice. (Although cold is the defining characteristic of the envi-

(continued on page 73)

A Canadian Gallery

Wearing a mixture of European, Canadian, and Indian-style garb, four fur traders enjoy a wintry smoke. Tobacco was regarded as an absolute necessity by les habitants *of Canada; on the rivers, the voyageurs measured distance in pipes.*

In the introduction to his published account of his two epic journeys through the Canadian wilderness, Alexander Mackenzie lamented that the haste with which he was required to travel—because of the shortness of the north country spring and summer, the undetermined but presumably lengthy distances he had to traverse, and his desire not to winter in country that was unknown to him—made it impossible to devote the appropriate measure of attention to the rugged and beautiful country through which he passed and to the numerous animals and native peoples that inhabited it. His prose, he cautioned readers, inadequately depicted these previously unknown regions; he was, by his own admission, not a "candidate for literary fame." And, of course, two such expeditions, conducted for business purposes, on the cheap, and of necessity with a certain amount of secrecy—the North West Company had no desire to inform its rivals about the explorations of its traders—could not, unlike later exploratory parties, employ artists to give visual form to Mackenzie's words. Many of the best artistic portrayals of the Canadian West were therefore rendered later than Mackenzie's explorations, but the forbiddingness of *le pays d'en haut* ensured that they portrayed a world not greatly changed from the one Mackenzie had known.

The Irish-born artist Paul Kane painted this portrait of François Lucie, a mixed-blood Cree Indian, in 1846. Although there was a great deal of exploitation in the fur trade, the traders were dependent on good relations with the Indians, who served them as guides, hunters, trappers, interpreters, cooks, tailors, friends, lovers, and spouses.

Another Kane portrait, this one of a full-blooded Cree he encountered at Fort Carlton, a Hudson's Bay Company (HBC) outpost on the North Saskatchewan River west of Cumberland House. The Cree were the most frequent trading partners of the Nor'Westers and the Bay men.

Ein Wilder von den Saulteux Indianern
am rothen Fluß.

A Salteaux Indian, as depicted by Peter Rindisbacher, who is notable today more for the documentary interest of his visual record of frontier life—in this case, the Indian's clothing—than for his artistic skill. A contemporary described Rindisbacher, who died in 1834 at the age of 28, as a "young Swiss artist who resided for some years on the frontier and attained a happy facility in sketching both the Indians and the wild animals."

Encampment River W

Neither Mackenzie nor his murderous mentor, Peter Pond, anticipated that their hypothetical river routes west were blocked by the formidable Canadian Rockies. This view is by Kane, who did most of his Canadian work in the course of two expeditions conducted under the auspices of the Hudson's Bay Company.

Voyageurs, traders, and Indians prepare their
night's encampment along the Winnipeg River,
one of the most well traveled of the Nor'Westers'
waterways. For the voyageurs, the canoe was both
conveyance and shelter; at night they would crawl
beneath an overturned vessel to sleep.

A brigade of HBC boats in full sail; the design on the sail of the vessel at center is an Ojibwa symbol of good luck. Because birch trees did not grow on the shores of Hudson Bay, the HBC men transported their goods and furs in York boats—40-foot, double-ended, flat-bottomed craft—rather than in canoes.

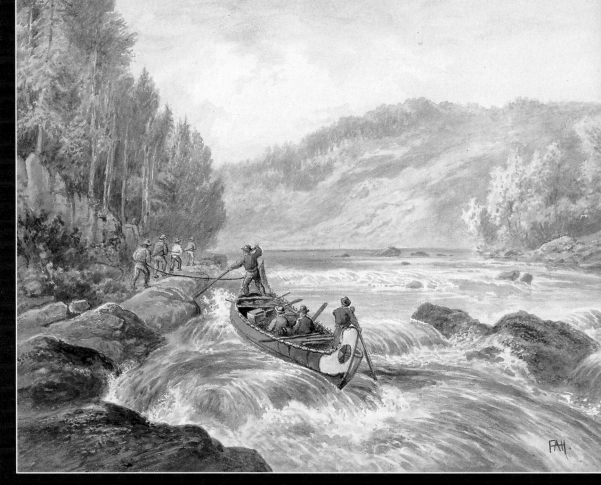

When the opposing current grew too strong, the
voyageurs stopped paddling and poled and towed
their simple yet ingenious craft instead. With such
unyielding determination—Perseverance, according
to the NWC motto—did Alexander Mackenzie
explore the Canadian West.

(continued from page 64)

ronment of the Canadian North at all times, it is worth
noting that Mackenzie was traveling during what mete-
orologists have termed the Little Ice Age. The journals of
explorers and fur traders from this period are filled with
details attesting to weather conditions exceptionally harsh
even for the normally frigid climate.) The prevailing north
wind had pushed ice floes to the south shore of the lake,
preventing Mackenzie from immediately pushing westward in search of the mouth of Pond's river.

Snow and icy rain soaked skins and dampened morale,
while ice hampered progress. It took Mackenzie and his
men seven entire days to cross to the north side of the
lake, which they reached by following a string of islands
that spanned its width. The crossing was laborious and
harrowing, with the constant prospect of disaster. Ice can
quickly tear the skin of a birchbark, and the vessels are
easily tipped, especially when navigating on a large lake.
On the far side of Great Slave Lake, strong winds and
currents almost drove the canoes onto the rocky shores
before they could find a safe place to land.

The tension of the crossing caused the first tempera-
mental outbursts from Mackenzie's party. Possibly the fear
of the unknown, which would become increasingly evident, was beginning to work on some, or perhaps they
were simply feeling the strain of overwork and constant
cold and damp. In any event, several quarrels occurred.
None were particularly significant in and of themselves,
except to the extent that dissension, among a small party
dependent to a high degree on cooperation, could threaten
the success and even the safety of the entire expedition.
A "very serious dispute" between two of the voyageurs was
resolved by Mackenzie by ignoring it, increasing the rum
ration that night, and allowing a couple of hours of extra
sleep in the morning; the problem soon solved itself.

Other disagreements were solved the same way. Mackenzie seems to have had a standoffish, even prickly personality, especially in his relations with those, like

voyageurs and Indians, whom he apparently regarded as his social inferiors. Nothing like the genuine bonds of friendship that came to join Samuel Hearne and Matonabbee, the Chipewyan chief who guided him to the Coppermine, is anywhere evident in Mackenzie's accounts of his travels. Even so, and although his companions were rarely mentioned by name in the published version of the journals he kept on his voyages, the manner in which his expeditions were conducted—rapid progress over extremely rugged, unmapped, and unknown terrain, with relatively little in the way of resentment or mutiny from his party, and no serious injuries or illness—attests to his skill as a leader. Evidently, he possessed some combination of qualities that induced people to follow him and perform at a high level of achievement as well as just the right mixture of foresight, daring, prudence, and luck to bring himself and his party through safely.

On the north shore of Great Slave Lake, not far from present-day Yellowknife, Mackenzie spent a long day trading with an eager band of Dogrib Indians. The furs he obtained, along with letters to cousin Roderick and the NWC controlling partners, were sent back with Leroux to Fort Chipewyan, but he was less successful in obtaining information about the whereabouts of the entry to Pond's river. One of the Dogrib was persuaded to hire on as a guide, but even so, Mackenzie and his men spent two frustrating weeks prowling through a maze of beaver ponds, mud flats, sandbars, and shallows at the lake's west end in search of the river. English Chief finally grew so frustrated that he threatened to slit the guide's throat. Unnerved by the Chipewyan's murderous intentions and by his belief in his tribe's legends about the monsters said to guard the entry to the "Big River," the now-reluctant guide sought to escape, and at night Mackenzie had to sleep on the tails of his coat to prevent him from slipping away. On June 29, at last, the river was found, and the expedition

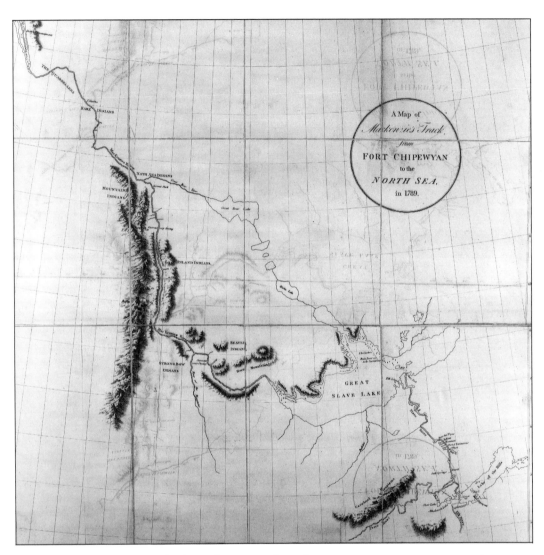

entered the Mackenzie, which at this point flowed westward, toward the ocean, just as Pond had said it would.

Although rain continued to soak him and his men to their skin, an air of optimism pervades Mackenzie's journal entries for this portion of the voyage. Several years later, in his introduction to the published edition of his journals, Mackenzie lamented that the haste with which he was required to proceed, as well as the various concerns of

A detail from a map of Mackenzie's journey from Fort Chipewyan down Pond's great river that appeared in his book about his explorations, Voyages from Montreal, on the River St. Laurence, Through the Continent of North America.

At Camsell Bend, Mackenzie received his first solid indication that his expedition would not go as planned—the Rocky Mountains loomed ahead of him, and the river veered from its westward course to the north.

leadership, made it impossible for him to linger in observation of the new country through which he was passing:

> These voyages, will not, I fear, afford the variety that may be expected from them. Mountains and vallies, the dreary waste, and wide-spreading forests, the lakes and rivers succeed each other in general description. . . . I could not stop to dig into the earth, over whose surface I was compelled to pass with rapid steps; nor could I turn aside to collect the plants which nature might have scattered on the way, when my thoughts were anxiously employed in making provision for the day that was passing over me.

Despite this disclaimer, he took careful note of the country near the entry to the Mackenzie, musing on the prospects for agriculture along the river—a habit perhaps adopted from Pond, who was well known for his experiments with raising potatoes and other vegetables at Athabasca—and recording the richness and texture of the soil, the thickness of the woodlands, the type of vegetation, and the abundance of game animals, especially the number of beavers and the quality of their fur. The expedition's hunters brought in a few beavers from small lakes not far away but very few from the areas closest to the river. Unfortunately for the expedition, the most frequently encountered animal was the dreaded mosquito, which found an ideal breeding ground on the melting tundra and muskeg. Mackenzie wrote that he and his men were "nearly suffocated by Swarms of Musquittoes."

One natural feature that Mackenzie, to his chagrin, could not avoid noticing was a range of "very high mountains"—the Canadian Rockies—extending north and south as far as one could see. Pond had believed that the mountains reached their northernmost extent at a point far south of the latitude of the Mackenzie; what he (and Mackenzie) had no way of knowing was that the great chain of stony peaks stretches all the way from the northernmost reaches of Alaska to New Mexico. Equally disconcerting for Mackenzie was that the river no longer coursed westward, toward the ocean, but veered northward at what is known today as Camsell Bend. He noted the change of direction and the appearance of the mountains in his journal but decided to continue on the river nonetheless, probably in the belief (or hope) that at some point the river would again swing toward the ocean and either cut a pass through the range to his west or pass to its north.

The northward swing and Mackenzie's hard driving did cause some consternation among his party. The voyageurs were somewhat accustomed to such a breakneck schedule, but the "Indians complain much of our hard marching, that they are not accustomed to such hard fatigue," according to Mackenzie, and he had to devote increased attention to cajoling them to continue. The uncertainty involved in navigating unknown waterways increased the tension. In their usual haunts, voyageurs would know every twist and turn of a stream, but on the uncharted Mackenzie, eternal vigilance was required. "We went very cautiously here expecting every moment that we would come to some great Rapid or Fall. We were so full of this that every person in his turn thought he heard a Noise and the falling of water which only subsisted in our Imaginations," reads a typical Mackenzie journal entry.

Mackenzie had to be concerned not only with the relations between himself and the Indian members of his own party but with those between his expedition and the various Indian bands it encountered along the river. Peaceful relations had to be maintained, both for the immediate safety of the expedition and so as to ensure the North West Company success in establishing the fur trade in the area. For the most part, Mackenzie's record with the Indians is admirable. There were few violent encounters, and his commerce with them was scrupulously honest, even if motivated by self-interest. "We are traders, and apart from more exalted motives, all traders are desirous of gain. Is it not self evident that we will manage our business with more economy by being on good terms with the Indians than if at variance?" was how a prominent HBC man, John McLoughlin, later explained the prevailing attitude of the fur traders toward the Indians.

Most of the Indians the expedition encountered were small groups of several families; most had probably never before seen white men. Aware that they might be frightened by the arrival of his party, Mackenzie usually sent his own guides ahead to make contact with these bands and communicate his peaceful intentions. Only then would the large trade canoe be brought into shore. To demonstrate their own desire for friendship, the Indians often presented the explorers with fish and game; Mackenzie reciprocated by offering gifts of cloth, colored beads, and other trinkets. When his hunters needed shirts, Mackenzie traded with the river Indians for new apparel; when his own guides carried off several items from an abandoned campsite, he insisted they leave articles of trade as payment.

Mackenzie's honesty was matched by that of the Indians, which impressed him greatly. The Indians were allowed to roam freely through the explorers' campsites and supplies; the only incident occurred when one hungry band tried to help themselves to dinner, although, as Mackenzie unwittingly recognized, the misunderstanding owed more to cultural beliefs than to criminal intent. "I suppose they think provision should be common property among all People," he wrote somewhat caustically, unconsciously recording a truth about Indian notions of hospitality and generosity.

The record Mackenzie compiled of the habits and customs of the Indians he encountered reveals other aspects of his cultural bias and shortsightedness as well as his skills as an observer. Before he even met any Indians on the river, Mackenzie was able to glean from the method of cutting trees at their abandoned campsites that they lacked iron tools—an observation that disturbed him because it indicated that they had had no contact with Cook's or any of the other European ships that had visited the Pacific Coast or with other Indians who had. In each village he visited, Mackenzie described Indian costumes and ceremonies, measured tools and weapons, and marveled at their meticulous quill embroidery and fine basketry, but he judged each group by the criteria of his own culture. He characterized the first Slave and Dogrib groups he encountered as sickly, dusty, and greasy as a result of their "dirty way of living" and was critical of them because their clothing seemed to serve purely functional aims—warmth and comfort—rather than purposes of adornment and "modesty." The more northerly groups were judged superior because they wore long pants instead of a simple covering around the middle. Although he deplored the effects of alcohol on the Indians and found those tribes to which it had not yet been introduced to be more affluent and industrious—"It will appear from the fatal consequences I have repeatedly imputed to the use of spiritous liquors, that I more particularly consider these people as having been, morally speaking, great sufferers from their communication with the subjects of civilized nations," he wrote—he did not hesitate to use rum as an item of trade with all the tribes that he encountered. Nor, despite the need for diplomacy, did he refrain from kidnapping individual Indians to serve as guides when various trade goods did not serve as sufficient inducement.

July 10 marked a critical point in the expedition. The river had continued its northward course; that day, after taking a latitude reading of almost 68° north (above the Arctic Circle), Mackenzie realized that it was not going to empty into the Pacific. The mountains were still "running to the Northward as far as we could see," Mackenzie wrote, "and it was evident that these waters emptied themselves into the Hyperborean Sea [the Arctic Ocean]." It was at this point that he termed his watercourse the "River of Disappointment." Virtually every member of the party urged him to turn back—food supplies were low, and the

(continued on page 82)

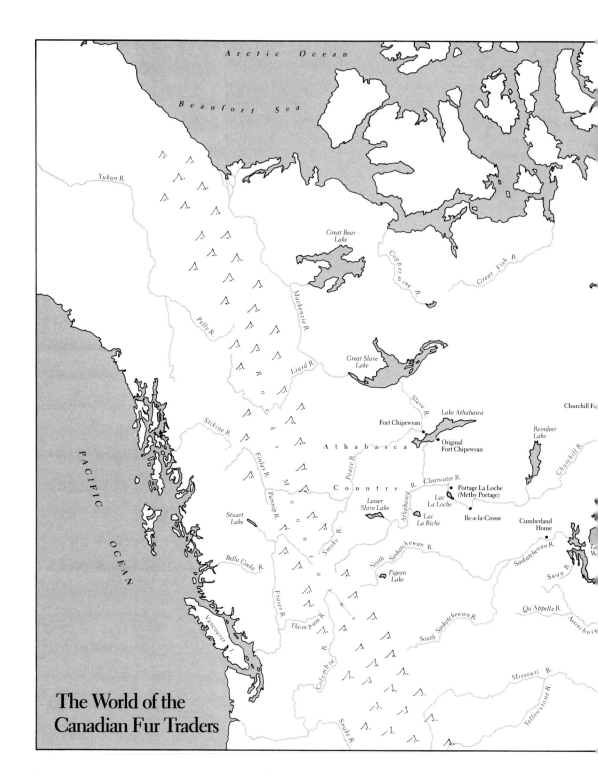

The World of the
Canadian Fur Traders

Western Canada was the
battlefield on which the Hudson's
Bay Company and the North
West Company fought for control
of the fur trade.

(continued from page 79)

party would be hard-pressed to reach Athabasca before the onset of winter—but Mackenzie prevailed upon them to continue, although he agreed that they would advance for just seven more days before reversing course. In persuading them, he recorded, he "did [not] fail to mention the courage and resolution which was the peculiar boast of the Northmen."

The Indians recognized that very evening that the ocean could not be far off when the expedition passed several deserted encampments with tent poles fashioned out of whalebones—a telltale sign that they had reached the land of their traditional enemies, the Inuit, as the native peoples of the Arctic are known. They pressed onward for several more days, wandering the puzzling channels of the river's delta, blocked from sight of the nearby ocean by small hills. On July 14, they camped on a large island in the river's mouth. That day, one of the men saw some large animals in the water; Mackenzie immediately recognized them as whales and named their campsite Whale Island. (It is known today as Garry Island.) That night, which was windless, the water rose and soaked their campsite. The only explanation could be a rising tide, and Mackenzie realized that they had reached the Arctic Ocean. With the true perseverance of the Nor'Wester, he had carried the expedition to its conclusion, but his regret at not having found what he was looking for—a passage to the Pacific—is palpable, recorded in the name he gave the river that he is credited with discovering.

The return journey began immediately. The expedition was now racing the onset of winter and traveling upriver, against the current. On some days, no progress at all could be made by paddling, and the men were forced to tow the canoes from shore with a rope. Even so, the party often made 30 miles in a day. This took quite a toll on their footwear; according to Mackenzie, the Indian women often spent all day sitting in the boats sewing moccasins, "as a pair does not last us above one Day." New paddles

This illustration of a native of the peninsula of Kamchatka, then part of Russia, appeared in the published edition of the journal of Captain James Cook. Pond had believed that where his great river emptied at Cook's Inlet was just a short ocean voyage from Russia, and Mackenzie carried Russian rubles in the event that he encountered Russians.

were also made constantly to replace those broken on rocks and submerged branches.

Despite his disappointment, Mackenzie still believed in the existence of a river flowing west to the sea, either through or beyond the mountains, and on the return journey he searched carefully for clues to its existence. At a Dogrib encampment, an Indian told English Chief of a large river on the other side of the mountains that led to a large "lake" where huge, evil men made enormous canoes and hunted "a kind of a large Beaver the Skin of which is almost Red." This was the kind of information Mackenzie was seeking; he believed the men to be Russian traders and the red-skinned beaver to be the sea otter. Although his journal entry betrays no excitement—his writing was relentlessly matter-of-fact—Mackenzie was almost certainly encouraged by the news. At a village farther upstream, an Indian drew a rough map that showed a fort near the mouth of a large river. Mackenzie interpreted this chart as showing Cook's River and a Russian fort that Pond had told him about called Unalaska. (Although his geography was erroneous, Pond was operating from a kernel of truth. The Russians had indeed made inroads in the Far Northwest—Mackenzie, in fact, carried Russian currency in the expectation that he would encounter them—but Unalaska was an outpost in the Aleutian Islands, a long distance from Cook's River, which was actually the inlet at whose upper end the present-day city of Anchorage, Alaska, now sits. For that matter, of course, the Pacific Ocean was some 1,000 miles farther away from Athabasca than Pond believed it to be.)

Encouraged by this news, Mackenzie decided to linger among the Indians for several days, hoping to learn more, a decision that provoked some unrest. Further interrogation provided only fantastic stories about cannibalistic men and strange animals, but as the rest of the party was eager to return home and worried about their safety, Mackenzie began to suspect his travel-weary interpreters of hiding pertinent details from him for fear that he would attempt further exploration that same season. The uneasiness among the explorers soon affected their relations with the villagers. A dispute arose between his hunters and the Indians over a canoe; Mackenzie shot a dog that had got loose and was rummaging among the supplies. That night, the Dogrib fled, but the abuses and dissension continued as the expedition made its way upriver. Mackenzie's men began stealing small items from the Indian camps and even tried to kidnap a young Indian girl, English Chief fought with a guide he accused of making advances to one of his wives, and the voyageurs began to argue among themselves.

By August 1, Mackenzie's interpreters hesitated to ask any detailed questions of the Indians they encountered, and English Chief flatly refused to scout for local camps. "They are still afraid that I may meet with the Natives who might give me Accounts of the other River and that I should go overland to it, and bring them along with me," Mackenzie wrote, and he decided to take one of the small Indian canoes and scout ahead himself.

But there was no one and nothing to find. Following the caribou on their late-summer migration to the forests, the Indians had deserted the river. Near Camsell Bend and beyond, the expedition encountered only abandoned campsites and empty trails. Undeterred, Mackenzie spent hours tracking Indians, without success, and near the bend he tried to climb a mountain in the hope of glimpsing the elusive western waterway from its peak. Unsuccessful, he was left with little choice but to head for Athabasca.

At Great Slave Lake, the weather, which had been favorable for some 300 miles, added to Mackenzie's disappointment. Once again, rain, at times turning to hail, pelted the explorers. While crossing the lake, the big canoe took in so much water it almost sank. A fortuitous rendezvous with Leroux on August 24 gave reason for lifted spirits, and Mackenzie ordered an increased ration of rum, but Leroux's report that he had obtained only eight packs of furs from the Indians—a quarter of what Mackenzie believed necessary to justify the establishment of a fort— only added to the Scotsman's frustration.

After paying off the Indians, who wished to remain at Great Slave Lake, with iron, tobacco, ammunition, and assorted trade goods, Mackenzie and the voyageurs hurried toward Athabasca, overcoming uncooperative weather— rain, hail, and sleet—their own fatigue, and the wreck of the big canoe during a portage. Finally, on the afternoon of September 12, through a lightly falling snow, they sighted Fort Chipewyan.

The Mackenzie, as it is now known, is the longest river in Canada, but its discoverer had no idea of its immensity when he first set out on it. This drawing of the river is by a later explorer of western Canada, George Back.

To the End
of the Continent

History would be kinder to Alexander Mackenzie than would the partners of the North West Company. At the summer gathering at Grand Portage in 1790, Mackenzie was disappointed but not surprised that his expedition was not hailed as a great triumph for the company. "My expedition is hardly spoken of, but this is what I expected," he wrote in a letter to Roderick. Although he had effectively doubled company territory, become the first to navigate and explore Canada's longest river, and discovered the more northerly expanses of the Rockies, he had not found a path to the Pacific, and based on Leroux's harvest and his own reports the region showed no great immediate potential in terms of fur. Nevertheless, Mackenzie's exploration was not seen as being totally without merit, for he was awarded an additional partnership share, giving him 2 of the NWC's 20. At his cousin's demand, Roderick was also made a partner. (The company's financial investment would prove not to have been misplaced. Between 1793 and 1805, the NWC would establish six profitable outposts on or near the Mackenzie.)

As he had demonstrated on the return journey from the Arctic, Mackenzie was now obsessed with finding a western route to the ocean. Exploration, not the business of running an NWC outpost, now constituted his chief interest. On his return to Fort Chipewyan, a chance meeting

Simon McTavish was the mastermind behind the North West Company, but he was not a strong booster of Alexander Mackenzie. The two would eventually have a falling-out over the direction of the North West Company.

at Cumberland House with Philip Turnor, an HBC surveyor, confirmed Mackenzie's suspicion that his chief failing as an explorer was his unfamiliarity with the various scientific means of taking measurements and establishing location. Mackenzie had done quite well in calculating his latitude, or north-south position, while on his River of Disappointment, but he had had no way of fixing his longitude, or position east-west, which involved a much more difficult set of astronomical observations and calculations. While spending the winter at Fort Chipewyan, Turnor became the first to affix the correct longitude of the NWC's Athabascan outpost—at 111° west—which proved, when compared with the longitudinal measurements established by Cook on the Pacific Coast, that the Nor'Westers were a lot farther from the ocean than they had imagined.

At Turnor's urging, Mackenzie determined to return to England to study astronomy and navigation as a means of preparing himself for a second try at the Pacific. Leaving Roderick with instructions to "make all inquiry possible" about river routes west, he sailed for London in 1791 and enrolled at Cambridge University, where he took courses in astronomy, navigation, mathematics, and geography; he also spent considerable time talking to fur merchants, read the published accounts of Cook's expeditions, and may even have tracked down some of the men who had sailed with Cook. When he returned to Fort Chipewyan in late summer of 1792, he brought with him several scientific instruments—a telescope, a sextant, a compass, a chronometer, and an azimuth—as well as knowledge of two methods of calculating longitude without a reliable timepiece. (With a portable clock able to keep accurate time on the water, of which there were very few in existence in the 1790s, determining longitude becomes a relatively simple measure.) Despite all this training, on his second journey Mackenzie would sometimes prove distrustful of scientific methods and would often use the time-

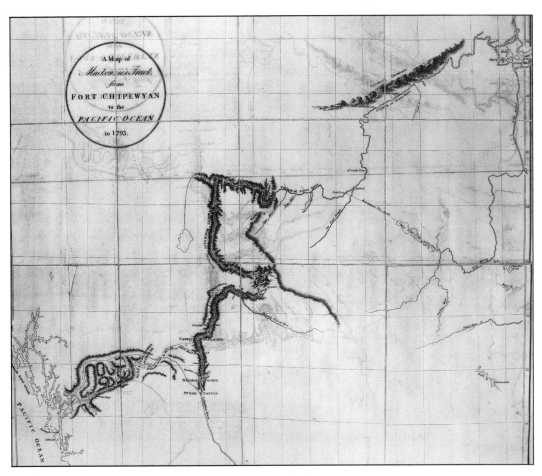

honored method of dead reckoning—through observation and intuition, simply estimate the distance traveled from a fixed point—to determine his location. Even so, his scientific measurements were reasonably accurate, and he often stayed awake late into the night in order to take celestial readings.

His plans had already been made. This time he would explore another of Pond's great rivers, the Peace, the course of which is westward, then south, and west again from its mouth at the northwest end of Lake Athabasca. On November 1, 1792, after paddling 250 miles upriver, Mackenzie arrived at what would become known as Fort

A detail from a map tracing the route of Mackenzie's second expedition that appeared in Voyages from Montreal.

Fork, a rude winter quarters being built for him about 6 miles down the Peace from its juncture with the Smoky River. There he would spend the winter while awaiting the spring breakup. For company he had the six voyageurs who would accompany him—Jacques Beauchamp, François Beaulieux, Baptiste Bisson, François Courtois, and, once again, Joseph Landry and Charles Ducette, as well as Alexander Mackay, a huge, fearless, energetic Scot who would serve as second in command. The fort also received regular visits from the local Indians, who belonged to two tribes Mackenzie had not previously encountered. Mackenzie called them the Beaver Indians and the Rocky Mountain Indians. The Beaver, he recorded, were notable for their skill as hunters—there were elk, caribou, and buffalo in the region—and he brought two of them along with him in that capacity.

Mackenzie's second expedition left Fort Fork on May 9, 1793. Along with a dog, described only as "large and friendly," the eight Europeans traveled in a large canoe designed by Mackenzie. Twenty-five feet long, 4 feet 9

A Rindisbacher drawing of an Indian hunting buffalo. The North West Company encouraged Indian hunters to kill buffalo in order to stock the company's many pemmican stations.

inches wide, and able to carry 3,000 pounds of goods, it was nonetheless light enough for only 2 men to carry. The Indians accompanied them in a smaller vessel that was abandoned at some point along the way.

Despite leaks in the larger vessel and freezing weather at night, the first 10 days of the journey were delightful. Uncharacteristically, Mackenzie was moved to wax rhapsodic about the beauty of the countryside:

> This magnificent theatre of nature has all the decoration which the trees and animals of the country can afford it: groves of poplars in every shape vary the scene; and their intervals are enlivened with vast herds of elks and buffaloes. . . . The whole country displayed an exuberant verdure.

He noted large stands of willow, alder, white spruce, and white birch suitable for making canoes, as well as likely sites for NWC outposts. The hunters, sometimes aided by the dog, brought in a number of elk and buffalo to eat, and at one point the party encountered the tracks of a kind of bear unknown to Mackenzie. "The Indians entertain a huge apprehension of this bear, which is called the grisly [grizzly] bear," he wrote, "and they never venture to attack it but in a party of three or four." He was more gratified to learn, from some Mountain Indians with whom the party camped on May 12, that they were just 10 days from the Rockies and that it was possible, by means of one day's portage from the Peace's south fork, to reach a "large river beyond the mountains." To his delight, the Rockies first came into view on May 17, their snowcapped peaks to the southwest providing a "very agreeable object."

Less pleasing were the rapids of the Canyon of the Peace, where the river forces its tortuous way between steep cliffs carved into the sides of mountains. For 10 days, Mackenzie and his men toiled through the canyon, alternately poling and towing the canoe from precarious footholds on the cliffs above, resorting to frequent portages,

As most voyageurs considered themselves more naturally "water dogs" than beasts of burden, they preferred sailing through the most dangerous rapids to making any sort of portage.

hauling the canoe up a precipitous path hacked through the forest on the mountainside. Rockslides constantly threatened to sweep the explorers from their hard-won footholds; the prickles of a tall cactuslike plant Mackenzie dubbed the "devil's club" tore their moccasins and ripped their feet to shreds. At night the explorers slept with their backs against tree trunks to protect themselves from rockslides and mud avalanches.

Beyond the canyon, the Peace's strong current slowed the expedition's progress, and the party was forced to stop frequently to repair the canoe (which had been badly damaged in the rapids), replace broken paddles, and dry their clothes and supplies. Heavy rains and frequent drenchings by the ice-cold river made the explorers miserable, and on at least one night they were disconcerted by the howling of a wolf prowling around their campsite. About 100 miles west of the canyon, the Peace forks as it enters the Rockies. All of the party, except for its leader, wanted to take the northern tributary, but Mackenzie, remembering what the Mountain Indians had told him, wanted to take the southern tributary—known today as the Parsnip—and his will prevailed. The strength of the Parsnip's current, which flows north and limited their progress on the first day to two or three miles, only increased his men's disgruntlement, but, wrote Mackenzie, using "arguments which were the best calculated to calm their immediate discontents . . . I delivered my sentiments in such a way as to convince them that I was determined to proceed."

The expedition was now entering the Rockies, and Mackenzie was desperately looking for the portage about which his Indian informant had told him. On June 9, the party came upon a small band of Sekani Indians, "the people of the rocks." At first, two Sekanis brandished their weapons threateningly, but Mackenzie's soothing tone convinced them to lay down their arms, and when he stepped ashore and took them by the hand, they became friendly. After much questioning, he was able to learn from them that they obtained metal tools from tribes that went down to a "stinking lake"—the Pacific Ocean—to trade with white men who sailed ships "as big as islands." One of the Sekani drew for him, using charcoal on a piece of bark, a map of a route to the great river—it required crossing a series of small lakes, portages, and a smaller river—that would take them to the sea.

After continuing for several days on the Parsnip, which gradually diminished until it was little more than a stream, the explorers entered the series of lakes the Sekani had described. The first, known today as Arctic Lake, was choked with driftwood and was so high from the spring melts that it had overflowed its banks, allowing the canoe to pass "among the branches of trees." At its far end, an Indian trail of, according to Mackenzie, exactly 817 paces led to another pond, now known as Pacific Lake. In crossing this trail, Mackenzie realized, he had traversed the Continental Divide—the crest of the Rockies and the separating point of the continent's river systems. On the far side of the divide, Mackenzie realized with delight as he watched two streams running down into Pacific Lake, the rivers would flow westward, toward the ocean. Mackenzie and his men were the first whites to cross the divide this far north.

The going did not immediately get easier. Scouts sent ahead reported that the waterway at Pacific Lake's far end was a "fearful detail of rapid currents, fallen trees, and fallen stones." Mackenzie dubbed it the Bad River, and it wasted little time living up to its moniker. On June 13, the canoe was caught in a fearful stretch of rapids that sent it careening from stony bank to stony bank. Huge boulders smashed its stern and tore its bottom out; the helmsman, desperate to slow the vessel's uncontrolled progress, made the mistake of grabbing hold of an overhanging tree, the elasticity of which caused it to bend and then, like a catapult, fling him head over heels onto the shore. By grabbing hold of the wrecked hull of the canoe and hanging on for

The Peace River, shortly before it reaches the Rockies. In the mountains, Mackenzie, relying on the advice given him by some Mountain Indians, took his party up the Peace's south fork, which is known today as the Parsnip River.

"Being endowed by nature with an inquisitive mind and an enterprising spirit; possessing also a constitution and frame of body equal to the most arduous undertakings, and being familiar with toilsome exertion in the pursuit of mercantile pursuits, I not only contemplated the practicability of penetrating across the continent of America, but was confident of [my] qualifications," wrote Mackenzie.

dear life, the rest of the party managed to avoid drowning, but the boat was badly damaged and the entire supply of musket balls had been swept overboard.

A day was devoted to drying supplies, soothing frayed nerves, and repairing the canoe; when the party resumed its travels, rapids and swamps necessitated much portaging. In the early-morning hours of June 17, the Sekani who had come with them as a guide deserted, but Mackay, scouting ahead, had already found what he believed to be the great river. That night, Mackenzie and his men "had the inexpressible satisfaction of finding ourselves on the bank of a navigable river, on the West side of the great range of mountains." After a day's rest, occasioned by torrential rain and the party's great fatigue, a short and easy jaunt on a smaller watercourse—the Macgregor—brought them to a powerful river that flowed beneath fir, spruce, and cedar trees and high white cliffs. This was the Fraser River, named years later after Simon Fraser, the Nor'Wester who in 1808 would become the first man to navigate its length, but to Mackenzie belongs the credit for its "discovery." (Of course, the native peoples of the region had always known of its existence.)

Often traveling through thick fog, the expedition continued to the southwest. Smoke, presumably from campfires, could be seen at irregular intervals; on June 19, as it rounded a bend in the river, the party surprised a band of Carrier Indians, who unleashed a volley of arrows and retreated. Farther downriver, the explorers examined a large abandoned lodge, fashioned from cedar, big enough to house three families and containing intricate equipment for catching fish. Pressing on, Mackenzie learned that the damage it had absorbed had at last made the canoe "so crazy" that a new bottom had to be fashioned for it; the next day, June 21, he ordered a 90-pound bag of pemmican cached for the return journey.

That same evening, after passing beneath cliffs of "blue and white clay" sculpted by nature into "grotesque shapes," the expedition came upon a Carrier encampment. Another hail of arrows greeted them, but after Mackenzie strategically positioned one of his Indian sharpshooters to cover him, he stepped ashore bearing "looking glasses, beads, and other alluring trinkets" as well as two pistols tucked into his belt. An understanding was quickly reached, and within a short time Mackenzie and his men were within the village, distributing glass beads to the women and sugar to the children.

The Fraser, Mackenzie would soon learn, was another river of disappointment. According to the Carrier, it was indeed of great length, and white men regularly came to its mouth in tremendous canoes with goods made of iron. But falls and rapids, "which poured between perpendicular rocks that were much higher, and more rugged, than any we had yet seen," made it unnavigable farther down, and along its banks lived several warlike tribes, armed with guns, who would not let them pass.

Nevertheless, Mackenzie and his men continued downriver for a day, until an encounter with another Indian of a different tribe, an old man, convinced him to reconsider. The old man confirmed what the Carrier had said about the Fraser, and he added details about the difficulty of its portages and the indirectness of its course. The Fraser, he said, did not head immediately westward toward the coast but flowed for a long distance southward before veering west. He recommended that the explorers abandon the river for an overland trail that headed directly west and was used by the Indians to reach the coast, where, after a journey of no more than six nights, "they meet the people who barter iron, brass, copper, beads . . . for dressed leather, and beaver, bear, lynx, fox and marten skins."

After a tense council with his men, who were discouraged at the prospect of backtracking and were persuaded only by his insistence that he would continue alone if necessary, Mackenzie led his men back upriver. Misunderstandings with the Carrier, who believed that the whites' return signified an intent to harm them, slowed the explorers for several days, as did the necessity of building a new canoe. On July 4, led by a Carrier guide, the party set out westward along an overland trail that paralleled the course of the West Road River (known also as the Blackwater). Each of the voyageurs carried on his back his gun and 90 pounds of supplies—pemmican, rice, corn, trade goods, ammunition, and scientific instruments. Mackay and Mackenzie carried 70 pounds each; the Indians, 45. The remaining supplies and the canoe were buried or concealed near the confluence of the Fraser and the West Road.

The explorers traveled the trail for two weeks, being passed from different bands of local Indians by their guides. On the first day, Mackenzie's anticipation was whetted by an encounter with an Indian who wore minted coins—one English, one from the state of Massachusetts—as pendants from his ears. That night he and his men were lulled to sleep by the soothing sound of the Indians singing, in hushed, plaintive tones that reminded them of hymns.

Succeeding days were more stressful, as the expedition climbed into the Coastal Range. The glare of sunlight off patches of snow caused sunburn and snow blindness, and the elevation brought light-headedness, headaches, increased fatigue, and difficulty in breathing—the symptoms of altitude sickness. Among the mountain tribes, Mackenzie was pleased to find more American coins and clothes made of sea otter fur. Near nightfall on July 17, after hours of climbing, the explorers crossed through a narrow pass—later named after Mackenzie—above the tree line. Far below them, in the distance, a river shimmered, and an Indian village was visible at the fringes of a thick woods of exceptionally tall pine, hemlock, and spruce trees that spread for miles. Though he agreed to his exhausted men's suggestion that they camp for the night, Mackenzie found himself unable to stop, and his men had no choice but to follow. Groping their way through the darkness, they made their way to the village, noticing as they did that the climate on this side of the mountains was cooler and wetter, allowing the trees to grow to tremendous proportions and supporting abundant wildlife, especially mountain goats.

News of the white men's journey had evidently preceded them, for they were welcomed without surprise and treated hospitably at both of the inhabited Bella Coola villages that they visited. Mackenzie gave the name Friendly Village to the first settlement—the one they had seen after crossing Mackenzie Pass—and called the second, better-populated settlement Great Village. In both he was impressed by the handsomeness of the people, the workmanship of their clothing—a robe, draped around the shoulders, clasped at the neck, and flowing nearly to the ground, made of finely worked cedar bark interwoven with sea otter fur and red and yellow threads—the comparative richness of the tribe compared with the mountain peoples, and the ingenuity of the technology they used to catch

At a length of up to 5 feet and weighing as much as 80 pounds, the sea otter is the largest of the otters. Throughout the 19th century, the sea otter was hunted so relentlessly for its fur that it was threatened with extinction. Since 1911, an international treaty has prohibited its killing.

A *native of Nootka Sound, on Vancouver Island, as drawn by one of the artists of the Cook expeditions. Cook's successful trade with the Nootka Sound natives inspired Pond's and Mackenzie's interest in the Northwest as well as the explorations of George Vancouver.*

salmon, their staple food, especially the large wooden weirs that spanned the Bella Coola River. He was complimentary as well about the Indians' architecture; the Bella Coola lived in large wooden lodges, 100 feet long by 40 feet wide; raised 10 to 12 feet above the ground on wooden poles as a protection against flooding, divided into familial sleeping quarters around a communal hearth and living area. Many of these lodges featured finely crafted cedar chests.

The workmanship of the Bella Coola was also evident in a 45-foot-long canoe that Mackenzie examined at Great Village. The vessel was painted black and decorated with the white figures of fish; sea otter teeth, which resemble their human counterparts, were imbedded along the gunwales. The Indians told them that about 10 years earlier they had gone in this vessel down to the ocean, where they encountered two ships and many white people, who treated them with great kindness. Mackenzie was certain that the reference was to the vessels and crew of Captain Cook, whose journals mentioned meeting Indians near this locale who adorned their canoes with "human" teeth.

Such news convinced Mackenzie that he was near his goal. With some Bella Coola guides, he and his men, using a borrowed canoe, pressed on to a third village, which was deserted but afforded them a resting place. From the porch of their lodge, they saw, for the first time, the Pacific Ocean, mingling with the waters of the Dean Channel of the Bella Coola River. The next day's travel brought them into an "arm of the sea," where they saw many sea otters and seals; it also brought a confrontation with a war party of Bella Bella warriors, about whose bellicosity they had been warned. The Bella Bella mentioned a recent attack by white men named Bensins and Macubah; although the reference baffled Mackenzie, it seems in retrospect that the Indians were referring to the British explorer George Vancouver, whose ships, in the process of surveying the Northwest, had put in there just a month earlier. The standoff continued until nightfall, at which point the Bella Bella retreated, but when they reappeared the next morning, Mackenzie decided that he had come far enough. He mixed some vermilion dye with grease paint and scrawled in large letters on the face of the boulder behind which his party had taken shelter: "Alexander Mackenzie, from Canada by land, the 22nd of July, 1793." With that, the party paddled hastily upriver ahead of their Bella Bella pursuers.

The return journey was made in great haste. In his published narrative, Mackenzie devotes just a small number of pages to the return. It had taken him and his men 74 days to cover the more than 1,200 miles to the coast, but it required only 33 days, over the same rugged terrain, to reach Fort Fork, even though most of the party was exhausted to the point of illness and Mackenzie had to be carried for several days because of painfully swollen ankles. Good fortune aided their return; all their caches were found intact, they were reunited with their dog—the curious creature had wandered off to do some exploring of his own during their stay with the Bella Coola—on the trail between Great and Friendly villages, and on emerging from the Canyon of the Peace in mid-August they found the weather unseasonably warm and the nearby plains teeming with buffalo and elk, which afforded them the opportunity to satisfy their long-denied appetite. (A 250-pound elk carcass yielded only 2 meals.) With shouts of celebration and the frenzied discharge of muskets, they arrived at Fort Fork on August 24, 1793.

Mackenzie's somewhat understated narrative served to downplay the hardships of the western passage, but the toll the journey had taken on him was quite evident that winter at Fort Chipewyan, where the usually indefatigable Scotsman succumbed to nervous exhaustion and suffered a breakdown. Eager to write up his report on the journey for the other NWC partners, he confided to Roderick that he was utterly unable to concentrate and spent most of his time in tortured reverie, plagued by strange dreams and visions. "I could not close my eyes without finding myself in company with the Dead," he wrote his cousin. Canada's wild north country had broken its foremost explorer. He resolved to leave le pays d'en haut forever. "I am more anxious now than ever," he confided to Roderick near the end of his winter of discontent. "For I think it unpardonable in any man to remain in this country who can afford to leave it. What a pretty Situation I am in this winter. Starving and alone, without the power of doing myself or any body else any Service."

But before he could leave the north country, he needed to settle with the NWC partners. The 1794 summer gathering at Grand Portage was a tumultuous affair. Mackenzie arrived determined to receive his due for his latest accomplishment, which had added much new territory to the NWC dominion, whereas the Montreal partners questioned the worth of an achievement that had cost the company much but had not yielded even one beaver fur. Even more troublesome was Mackenzie's advocacy of the

Bella Coola Indians engage in a masked dance. According to Mackenzie, the Bella Coola were "altogether dependent on the sea and rivers for their sustenance" and were the "most susceptible of civilization" of all the Indians he encountered.

complaints of the wintering partners, who believed they were being shortchanged in the partnership agreement and were having difficulty doing business because of the inferiority of the trade goods they were receiving from Montreal. The single greatest cause of controversy, however, was Mackenzie's contention that the North West Company should expand its trade to the Pacific by establishing a harbor on the coast, accessible by the route he had pioneered; by so doing, the company could exploit the growing trade with China and the rest of Asia. The crucial corollary to this proposal, which Mackenzie presented to such important figures as the lieutenant governor of upper Canada and the governor in chief of British North America, in addition to the Montreal partners, was that the North West Company should merge with the Hudson's Bay Company. The entire massive operation would be run from London, with its most important New World hubs located on Hudson Bay and the Pacific Coast.

Although he recognized its merits, the plan enraged McTavish, who saw in it the means to eliminate Montreal's—and his—control of the fur trade. The result was a falling-out between the NWC's founder and dominant figure and its most famous trader. (Despite the Montrealers' carping, Mackenzie's discovery of a route to the ocean had greatly enhanced his prestige, especially among the wintering partners, who above all admired endurance, fortitude, and perseverance.) Mackenzie was voted a third partnership share and left Athabasca forever. He spent some time in London, more in Montreal—it was at this point that he joined the raucous Beaver Club—and a period in New York City, where he was sent as the NWC's agent, but he continued to chafe at McTavish's resistance to his plans, especially once he learned that American fur-trading concerns were making plans to exploit the Pacific Northwest.

The break came at the Grand Portage get-together in 1799. Mackenzie's partnership agreement had run its course, and he announced that he would be leaving the company. The wintering partners sent up a clamor protesting his resignation and passed a motion avowing that Mackenzie alone, of the five controlling partners, enjoyed their confidence. Throughout the brouhaha, McTavish remained silent; irate and disappointed, Mackenzie left the Great Hall. His days as a Nor'Wester were over. His place as partner was taken by Roderick, whose ascension caused a breach between the two cousins that lasted for five years.

Although unappreciated by some of his former partners, Mackenzie was lionized in London, to which he returned after a short stay in Montreal. He was hailed as the conquering explorer of the New World wilderness, had his likeness done by the king's portrait painter, and in 1802 was knighted, just several months after the publication of his account of his adventures. *Voyages from Montreal, on the River St. Laurence, Through the Continent of North America, to the Frozen and Pacific Oceans in the Years 1789 and 1793; With a Preliminary Account of the Rise, Progress, and Present State of the Fur Trade of That Country* was an influential best-seller, despite its daunting title. Among its readers were France's emperor Napoléon Bonaparte, who examined it for insights as to how he might best damage English interests in the North American West, and U.S. president Thomas Jefferson, whose reading informed his direction of the famous transcontinental exploratory expedition of Meriwether Lewis and William Clark. (Upon reaching the Pacific from St. Louis, Clark, in conscious imitation of Mackenzie, etched in a pine tree the words "William Clark December 3rd 1805. By Land from the U. States in 1804 & 1805.")

Mackenzie might have left the Canadian West behind, but he had not abandoned the fur trade. From London and during his frequent visits to Montreal, he presided over the reorganization of the New North West Company (commonly known as the XY Company for the insignia that marked its goods) into Alexander Mackenzie & Co., a fur-trading concern whose Montreal-Athabasca operations soon placed it in murderous competition with the NWC. The XY traders built forts right next to the NWC outposts, plied the same rivers and waterways, and wooed the same Indians with brandy, rum, and trade goods; if possible, they were even more persevering and undaunted than the Nor'Westers, who referred to them nonetheless as "potties," from a French colloquialism meaning "men of putty." The rivalry between the two companies quickly descended into violence, with robbery and even murder not uncommon. By 1802, the XY Company, with fewer than half the NWC's 1,058 employees and 117 outposts, boasted an equal amount of working capital, and Mackenzie was engaged in secret bargaining to buy the Hudson's Bay Company.

Those negotiations failed, but in 1804 McTavish died, and his successor, Mackenzie's old drinking buddy Wil-

William McGillivray replaced Simon McTavish as head of the North West Company in 1804 following McTavish's death. Several years earlier, McTavish and Mackenzie had quarreled bitterly. According to the trader Alexander Henry, "The cause . . . was who should be the first—McTavish or Mackenzie, and as there could not be two Caesars in Rome, one must remove."

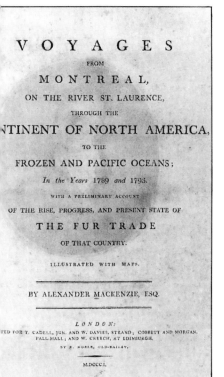

VOYAGES

FROM

MONTREAL,

ON THE RIVER ST. LAURENCE,

THROUGH THE

NTINENT OF NORTH AMERICA,

TO THE

FROZEN AND PACIFIC OCEANS;

In the Years 1789 and 1793.

WITH A PRELIMINARY ACCOUNT

OF THE RISE, PROGRESS, AND PRESENT STATE OF

THE FUR TRADE

OF THAT COUNTRY.

ILLUSTRATED WITH MAPS.

BY ALEXANDER MACKENZIE, ESQ.

LONDON:

TED FOR T. CADELL, JUN. AND W. DAVIES, STRAND; COBBETT AND MORGAN,
PALL-MALL; AND W. CREECH, AT EDINBURGH.

BY R. NOBLE, OLD-BAILEY.

M.DCCCI.

The title page to the original edition of Mackenzie's account of his two expeditions of exploration. According to the historian W. Kaye Lamb, Mackenzie was responsible for forming the "basis of a network on which Canada still depends for its economic survival."

liam McGillivray, immediately approached the XY Company about a merger. The NWC partnership agreement was again revamped, this time to permit the allocation of a quarter of its stock to the XY partners. But the completion of the merger was accompanied by a bitter irony; both sides, fearing his dominant personality, agreed that Mackenzie would not have an active role in the new partnership.

The explorer retired to Scotland, where in 1812, at the age of 48, he married Geddes Mackenzie, his beautiful 14-year-old cousin, with whom he had 2 sons and a daughter. He lived thereafter in baronial splendor on an estate near Moray Firth, purchased with his book and fur-trade earnings, which were considerable, trying to keep abreast of events in Canada. In his last known letter, to Roderick, he complained that the only news he received came from the newspapers, and he lamented the declining state of his health, which he attributed to the rigors of his life in the Canadian West. "I have at last been overtaken with the consequences of my life in the North West," he wrote. In 1820, he was taken ill while traveling by stagecoach from Edinburgh to Rosset and died in a roadside inn, probably as the result of the cumulative effects of a progressive kidney disorder.

The very next year, the North West Company merged with the Hudson's Bay Company under the latter's name, giving the HBC control of a fur and land empire, protected by royal charter, that reached from Montreal to Hudson Bay to Athabasca to the Pacific Northwest. The intensity of their climate and the sheer immensity and remoteness of the western regions ensured that significant settlement would not occur there until near the end of the 19th century, after the completion of the Canadian Pacific Railway, making it all the more remarkable that their northernmost and westernmost expanses were first explored 100 years earlier by a small number of persevering individuals in flimsy birch-bark canoes, foremost among them Alexander Mackenzie.

Further Reading

Bond, Rowland. *The Original Northwester—David Thompson*. Nine Mile Falls, WA: Spokane House, 1970.

Campbell, Marjorie W. *The Northwest Company*. New York: St. Martin's Press, 1957.

Daniells, Roy. *Alexander Mackenzie and the Northwest*. London: Faber and Faber, 1969.

Haworth, Paul L. *Trailmakers of the Northwest*. Toronto: Goodchild, 1921.

Innis, Harold. *The Fur Trade in Canada*. New Haven: Yale University Press, 1930.

———. *Peter Pond: Fur Trader and Adventurer*. Toronto: Goodchild, 1930.

Lamb, W. Kaye, ed. *Journals and Letters of Sir Alexander Mackenzie*. London: Cambridge University Press, 1970.

MacKay, Douglas. *The Honourable Company*. New York: Tudor, 1938.

Mackenzie, Alexander. *Alexander Mackenzie's Voyage to the Pacific Ocean in 1793*. New York: Citadel Press, 1963.

Mirsky, Jeanette. *The Westward Crossings*. London: Jarold and Sons, 1951.

Newman, Peter C. *Caesars of the Wilderness: The Story of the Hudson's Bay Company*. New York: Penguin Books, 1988.

———. *Company of Adventurers: The Story of the Hudson's Bay Company*. New York: Penguin Books, 1985.

Phillips, Paul C. *The Fur Trade*. Volume 2. Norman: University of Oklahoma Press, 1961.

Rich, E. E. *The Fur Trade and the Northwest to 1857*. Toronto: McClelland and Stewart, 1967.

Sheppe, Walter, ed. *First Man West*. Berkeley: University of California Press, 1962.

Smith, James K. *Alexander Mackenzie, Explorer: The Hero Who Failed*. Toronto: McGraw-Hill Ryerson, 1973.

Tanner, Ogden. *The Old West: The Canadians*. Alexandria, VA: Time-Life Books, 1977.

Twaites, R. G. *Peter Pond's Journal*. Madison: Wisconsin Historical Collection, 1908.

Vail, Phillip. *The Magnificent Adventures of Alexander Mackenzie*. New York: Dodd, Mead, 1964.

Vandiver, Clarence A. *The Fur Trade and Early Western Exploration*. Cleveland: Clarke, 1929.

Wagner, Henry R. *Peter Pond, Fur Trader and Explorer*. New Haven: Yale University Press, 1955.

Warkenstein, John, ed. *The Western Interior of Canada*. Toronto: McClelland and Stewart, 1964.

Wollacot, Arthur P. *Mackenzie and His Voyageurs*. London: Dent and Sons, 1927.

Wrong, Hume. *Sir Alexander Mackenzie, Explorer and Fur Trader*. Toronto: Macmillan, 1927.

Yerbury, J. Colin. *The Subarctic Indians and the Fur Trade, 1680–1860*. Vancouver: University of British Columbia Press, 1986.

Chronology

Entries in roman refer directly to Alexander Mackenzie and the exploration of Canada; entries in italic refer to important historical and cultural events of the era.

1670   *King Charles II of England grants the Hudson's Bay Company a virtual monopoly on the fur trade in the Hudson Bay region, an area of 1.5 million square miles in present-day Canada and the United States; the HBC soon establishes a network of fortified trading posts, called "factories" or "houses"*

1690   HBC trader Henry Kelsey explores the Saskatchewan River and becomes the first white man to view the Canadian prairie

1740   Explorer and trader Peter Pond born to a Scottish family in Milford, Connecticut

1750–80   Numerous independent traders, mainly French Canadian and Scottish, threaten the HBC fur monopoly; many of the independent traders join together to form the North West Company

1763   *France surrenders its territory in Canada to Great Britain*

1764   Alexander Mackenzie is born in the Outer Hebrides islands of Scotland

1774   Samuel Hearne establishes Cumberland House, the first inland HBC outpost

1775   Mackenzie's family moves to North America; *American Revolution begins*

1778   Peter Pond explores the region near Lake Athabasca; *Captain James Cook visits Nootka Sound and discovers a freshwater inlet in the vicinity of present-day Anchorage, Alaska*

1779   Mackenzie begins working for Finley, Gregory & MacLeod, a fur-trading company; Peter Pond becomes a partner in the North West Company

1785   Finley, Gregory & MacLeod merges with the North West Company; Mackenzie becomes a minor partner in the new firm

1787–88	Mackenzie winters with Pond in Athabasca; Pond tells him of a supposed lake and river route linking Athabasca and the Pacific
June–Sept 1789	Believing it to be Pond's "great river of the West," Mackenzie and a small party of voyageurs and Indians travel the length of Canada's longest river
1791	Mackenzie enrolls in Cambridge University to study navigation and astronomy in preparation for another journey westward
May 1793	Mackenzie sets out westward up the Peace River
June 1793	In the Rocky Mountains, Mackenzie makes the northernmost crossing to date of the Continental Divide
July 1793	On the advice of the Carrier Indians, Mackenzie and his entourage abandon the Fraser River for an overland route toward the Pacific, which they reach on July 22
Winter 1793–94	Exhausted from his travels, Mackenzie suffers a nervous breakdown at Fort Chipewyan and resolves to leave the north country
Summer 1794	Tensions develop between Mackenzie and the other NWC partners when he urges the establishment of a Pacific post and a merger with the HBC to facilitate Asian fur trade; Mackenzie leaves western Canada permanently
1799	His partnership agreement expired, Mackenzie resigns from the NWC and returns to London, where he is hailed as a hero
1802	Mackenzie is knighted by the British government after the publication of an influential book about his travels
1812	Mackenzie marries his young cousin and retires to Scotland
1820	Mackenzie dies in a Scottish roadside inn after years of declining health
1821	The HBC and the NWC merge under the former's name, creating an enormous fur and land empire that spans the continent from Montreal to the Pacific Northwest

Index

Picture Credits

George Back/National Archives of Canada/neg. # C93016: p. 85; Captain James Cook "A Voyage to the Pacific Ocean," Rare Book and Manuscript Division, New York Public Library, Astor, Lenox and Tilden Foundation: pp. 83, 97, 98; William Daniell, Museum Nan Eilean, Stornoway Isle of Lewis: p. 26; Collection of Glenbow Museum, Calgary, Alberta: p. 32; Samuel Hearne "A Journey from Prince of Wales Fort," Rare Book and Manuscript Division, New York Public Library, Astor, Lenox and Tilden Foundation: pp. 38, 40, 41; Frances Anne Hopkins/National Archives of Canada/ neg. # C2771: p. 53; Hudson's Bay Company Archives, Provincial Archives of Manitoba: pp. 29, 30; Baron La Hontan "New Voyages to North America," Rare Book and Manuscript Division, New York Public Library, Astor, Lenox and Tilden Foundation: p. 62; Paul Kane, Courtesy Royal Ontario Museum, Toronto: pp. 92, 100; John Lambert "Travels Through Canada and the United States," Rare Book and Manuscript Division, New York Public Library, Astor, Lenox and Tilden Foundation: p. 58; Thomas Lawrence/National Gallery of Canada, Ottawa: cover, p. 12; Alexander Mackenzie "Voyages from Montreal," Rare Book and Manuscript Division, New York Public Library, Astor, Lenox and Tilden Foundation: cover, pp. 75, 89, 94, 104; McCord Museum of Canadian History, Montreal: pp. 44–45, 50, 65; National Archives of Canada: pp. 23 (neg. # C8711), 49 (neg. # C99255), 86 (neg. # C164), 93 (neg. # C21296), 103 (neg. # C167); Courtesy National Archives of Quebec: p. 60; Public Record Office, Kew Richmond, Surrey UK, co. 700/American North and South 49: pp. 20–21; Sir John Richardson "Rocky Mountains at the Bend of the Mackenzie River," Arents Collection S1160, Rare Book and Manuscript Division, New York Public Library, Astor, Lenox and Tilden Foundation: p. 76; Peter Rindisbacher, Hudson's Bay Company Collection, Parks Canada, Lower Fort Garry National Park: p. 90; Peter Rindisbacher/National Archives of Canada: pp. 35 (neg. # C-001917), 67 (neg. # C1931); Rogers/National Archives of Canada: pp. 24 (neg.# 750), 42 (neg. # C16859); Royal Ontario Museum, Toronto: pp. 68, 70–71, 72; Claude Joseph Sauthier, Engraved by William Faden/National Archives of Canada/neg. # 7300: p. 14; Coke Smythe/ National Archives of Canada/neg. # C1026: p. 56; Stark Museum of Art, Orange Texas: pp. 66, 68–69; Sempronius Stretton/National Archives of Canada/neg. # 14817: p. 17; H. S. Watson/National Archives of Canada/neg. # C15244: p. 57

Georgia Xydes holds a masters degree in American civilization from the University of Texas at Austin. She has taught college courses in Germany and Japan as well as at her alma mater and the University of Texas at San Antonio.

William H. Goetzmann holds the Jack S. Blanton, Sr., Chair in History at the University of Texas at Austin, where he has taught for many years. The author of numerous works on American history and exploration, he won the 1967 Pulitzer and Parkman prizes for his *Exploration and Empire: The Role of the Explorer and Scientist in the Winning of the American West, 1800–1900*. With his son William N. Goetzmann, he coauthored *The West of the Imagination*, which received the Carr P. Collins Award in 1986 from the Texas Institute of Letters. His documentary television series of the same name received a blue ribbon in the history category at the American Film and Video Festival held in New York City in 1987. A recent work, *New Lands, New Men: America and the Second Great Age of Discovery*, was published in 1986 to much critical acclaim.

Michael Collins served as command module pilot on the *Apollo 11* space mission, which landed his colleagues Neil Armstrong and Buzz Aldrin on the moon. A graduate of the United States Military Academy, Collins was named an astronaut in 1963. In 1966 he piloted the *Gemini 10* mission, during which he became the third American to walk in space. The author of several books on space exploration, Collins was director of the Smithsonian Institution's National Air and Space Museum from 1971 to 1978 and is a recipient of the Presidential Medal of Freedom.

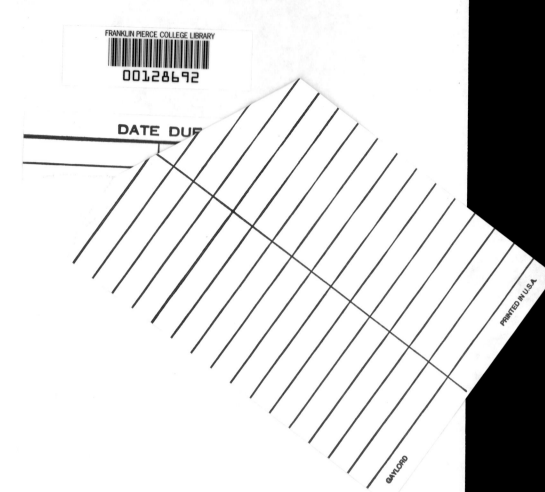